Joseph Ritson, Dorothea Ruggles-Brise, John Glen

Scotish Songs

Volume 1

Joseph Ritson, Dorothea Ruggles-Brise, John Glen

Scotish Songs
Volume 1

ISBN/EAN: 9783337181611

Printed in Europe, USA, Canada, Australia, Japan

Cover: Foto ©Thomas Meinert / pixelio.de

More available books at **www.hansebooks.com**

Scotish Songs

IN TWO VOLUMES

VOLUME THE SECOND

Glasgow
HUGH HOPKINS
1869

EDINBURGH:
PRINTED BY BALLANTYNE AND COMPANY,
PAUL'S WORK.

SONG XX.*

To the Tune of "Tak your Auld Cloak about you."

Get up, gudewyfe, don on your claise,
    And to the market make you boune,
'Tis lang tyme since your neighbours raise,
    They're weel nigh gotten unto the towne:
See you don on your better gowne,
    And gar the lasse big on the fyre;
Dame, doe not looke as ye wad frowne,
    But doe the thing whilk I desyre.

I speere what haist ye hae, gudeman,
    Your mither stay'd till ye war borne;
Wad ye be at the tother can,
    To scoure your throat so sune this morne?
Gude faith, I haud it but a scorne,
    That yee sud with my rising mel;
For when ye have baith said and sworne,
    I'l do but what I like mysel.

Gudewyfe, we maun needs have a care
    Sae lang's we wun in neighbours' rawe,
On neighbourhood to tak a share,
    And rise up when the cocke does crawe;

---

* This song is entitled in the manuscript, from which it is elsewhere mentioned to be given, "a Scotch brawle." The orthography is not everywhere that of the original, owing to the manifest ignorance or affectation of the English copyist.

T

For I have harde an auld said sawe,
   They that rise the last big on the fire,
What wind or weather soever blawe;
   Dame, do the thing quilke I desire.

Nay, what do ye talk of neighbourhood,
   Gif I lig in my bed while noone,
By nae man's shins I bake my bread,
   And ye need not reck what I hae done;
Nay, luik to th' clouting o' yer shoone,
   And with my rising do not mel,
For gin ye lig baith sheets abone,
   I'l do but what I wil mysel.

Gudewife, we maun needs tak a care,
   To save the geer that we hae won,
Or laye away baith plow and carre,
   And hang up Ring* when all is done:
Then may our bairnes a-begging runne,
   To seeke their mister in the myre,
So fair a thread as we hae spun,
   Dame, do the thing that I require.

Gudeman, ye may weel a-begging gang,
   Ye seeme sae weel to beare the poake,
Ye may as weel gang sune as syne,
   To seeke your meat amang gude folk;
In ilka house yese get a loake,
   When ye come whar yer gossips dwell:—
Nay, lo you luke sae like a gowke,
   I'l do but what I list mysel.

      * The dog.

Gudewyfe, you promised, when we were wed,
    That ye wad me truly obey,
Sir John can witness what you said,
    And I 'l go fetch him in this day ;
And gif that haly man will say
    Yese do the thing that I desyre,
Then sal we sune end up this fray ;
    Dame, do the thing that I require.

I nowther care for John nor Jacke,
    I 'l tak my leisure at myne ease,
I care na what you say a placke,
    You may go fetch him gin ye please ;
And gin ye want ane of a mease,
    You may eene gae fetch the deele in hell ;
Nay, I wad you wad let your japin cease,
    For I 'l do but quhat I like mysel.

Wel, since it wil nae better bee,
    I 'l tak my share or all be gane ;
The warst card in my hand sal flee,
    And, ifaith, I wat I can shifte for ane :
I 'l sel the plow, and lay to wadd the waine,
    And the greatest spender sal beare the bell :
And than, when all the goods are gane,
    Dame, do the thing ye list yoursel.

SONG XXI.

GET UP AND BAR THE DOOR.

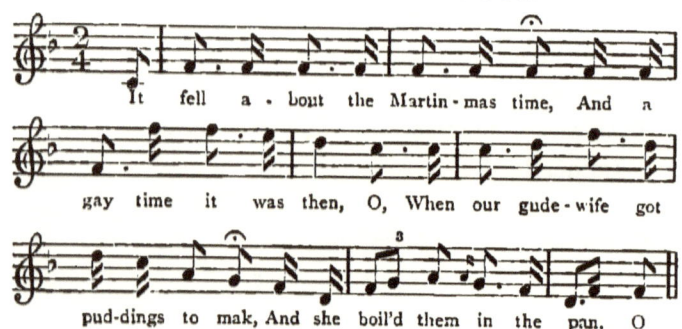

It fell about the Martinmas time, And a gay time it was then, O, When our gudewife got puddings to mak, And she boil'd them in the pan, O

The wind sae cauld blew south frae north,
   And blew into the floor, O:
Quoth our gudeman to our gudewife,
   "Gae out and bar the door, O."

"My hand is in my hussy'f skap,
   Gudeman, as ye may see, O,
An it shouldna be barr'd this hunder year,
   It's no be barr'd for me, O."

They made a paction 'tween them twa,
   They made it firm and sure, O;
That the first word whae'er should speak,
   Should rise and bar the door, O.

Then by there came twa gentlemen,
   At twelve o'clock at night, O,
And they could neither see house nor ha',
   Nor coal nor candle light, O.

"Now, whether is this a rich man's house?
   Or whether is it a poor, O?"
But never a word wad ane o' them speak,
   For the barrin' of the door, O.

And first they ate the white puddings,
   And then they ate the black, O;
Tho' muckle thought the gudewife to hersel,
   Yet ne'er a word she spak', O.

Then said the ane unto the ither,
   "Here, man, tak ye my knife, O,
Do ye tak aff the auld man's beard,
   And I'll kiss the gudewife, O."

"But there's nae water in the house,
   And what shall we do than, O?"
"What ails ye at the pudding broo,
   That boils into the pan, O?"

O up then started our gudeman,
   An angry man was he, O;
"Will ye kiss my wife before my een,
   And scad me wi' pudding bree, O?"

Then up and started our gudewife,
   Gied three skips on the floor, O;
"Gudeman, ye've spak the foremost word,
   Get up and bar the door, O."

SONG XXII.

DRUCKEN WIFE O' GALLOWAY.

Doun in yon mea-dow a cou-ple did tar-ry, The gude-wife she drank nae-thing but sack and ca-na-ry; The gude-man complain'd to her friends right sair-ly, Oh gin my wife wad drink hoo-ly and fair-ly. [Hoo-ly and fair-ly, hoo-ly and fair-ly, Oh gin my wife wad drink hoo-ly and fair-ly.]

First she drank Crommy, and syne she drank Gairie,
And syne she drank my bonnie grey marie,
That carried me thro' a' the dubs and the lairie.
    Oh gin my wife, &c.

She drank her hose, she drank her shoon,
And syne she drank her bonnie new gown;
She drank her sark that cover'd her rarely.
    Oh gin my wife, &c.

Wad she drink but her ain things, I wadna care,
But she drinks my claes that I canna weel spare;
When I'm wi' my gossips, it angers me sairly.
    Oh gin my wife, &c.

My Sunday's coat she's laid it a wad,
The best blue bonnet e'er was on my head;
At kirk and at market I'm covered but barely.
    Oh gin my wife, &c.

My bonnie white mittens I wore on my hands,
Wi' her neighbour's wife she has laid them in pawns;
My bane-headed staff that I lo'ed sae dearly.
    Oh gin my wife, &c.

I never was for wrangling nor strife,
Nor did I deny her the comforts of life,
For when there's a war, I'm aye for a parley.
    Oh gin my wife, &c.

When there's ony money, she maun keep the purse;
If I seek but a bawbee, she'll scold and she'll curse;
She lives like a queen, I but scrimped and sparely.
    Oh gin my wife, &c.

A pint wi' her cummers I wad her allow,
But when she sits down, she gets hersel fou,
And when she is fou she is unco camstairie.
    Oh gin my wife, &c.

When she comes to the street, she roars and she rants,
Has nae fear o' her neighbours, nor minds the house
    wants ;
She rants up some fule sang, like, Up yer heart, Charlie.
    Oh gin my wife, &c.

When she comes hame she lays on the lads,
The lasses she ca's baith b——s and j——s,
And ca's mysel' aye an auld cuckold carlie.
    Oh gin my wife, &c.

SONG XXIII.

OUR GUDEMAN CAM' HAME AT E'EN.

Our gude-man cam' hame at e'en, And hame cam' he; And
there he saw a sad-dle horse, Where nae horse should be. Oh
how cam' this horse here? How can this be? How cam' this
horse here, With-out the leave o' me? A horse, quo' she: Ay, a
horse, quo' he. Ye blind auld do-tard carle, And blind-er

SCOTISH SONGS.

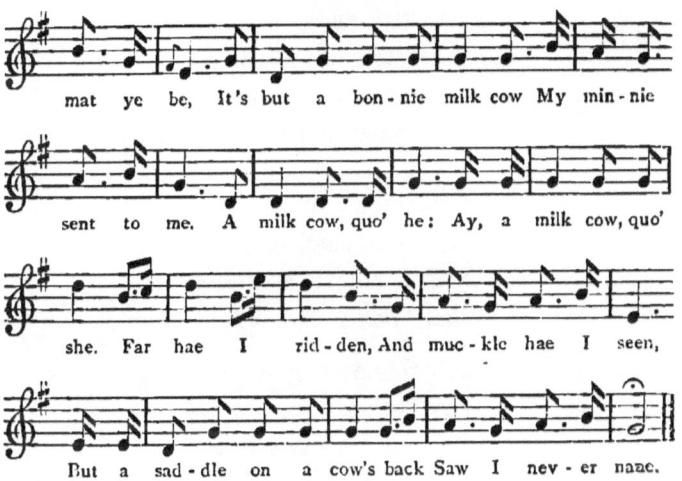

mat ye be, It's but a bon-nie milk cow My min-nie sent to me. A milk cow, quo' he: Ay, a milk cow, quo' she. Far hae I rid-den, And muc-kle hae I seen, But a sad-dle on a cow's back Saw I nev-er nane.

Our gudeman cam' hame at e'en,
    And hame cam' he;
He spied a pair of jackboots,
    Where nae boots should be.

What's this now, gudewife?
    What's this I see?
How cam' these boots there
    Without the leave o' me?

Boots! quo' she:
    Ay, boots, quo' he.
Shame fa' your cuckold face,
    And ill mat ye see,
It's but a pair of water stoups
    The cooper sent to me.

Water stoups! quo' he:
    Ay, water stoups, quo' she.

Far hae I ridden,
  And farer hae I gane,
But siller spurs on water stoups
  Saw I never nane.

Our gudeman cam' hame at e'en,
  And hame cam' he;
And there he saw a siller sword,
  Where nae sword should be:

What's this now, gudewife?
  What's this I see?
O how cam' this sword here,
  Without the leave o' me?

  A sword! quo' she:
    Ay, a sword, quo' he.
Shame fa' your cuckold face,
  And ill mat you see,
It's but a parridge spurtle
  My minnie sent to me.

  A parridge spurtle! quo' he:
    Ay, a parridge spurtle, quo' she.
Weel, far hae I ridden,
  And muckle hae I seen;
But siller-handed parridge spurtles
  Saw I never nane.

Our gudeman cam' hame at e'en,
  And hame cam' he;
There he spied a powder'd wig,
  Where nae wig should be.

What's this now, gudewife?
  What's this I see?
How cam' this wig here,
  Without the leave o' me.

    A wig! quo' she:
    Ay, a wig, quo' he.
Shame fa' your cuckold face,
  And ill mat you see,
It's naething but a clocken hen
  My minnie sent to me.

    A clocken hen! quo' he:
    Ay, a clocken hen, quo' she.
Far hae I ridden,
  And muckle hae I seen,
But powder on a clocken hen
  Saw I never nane.

Our gudeman cam' hame at e'en,
  And hame cam' he;
And there he saw a muckle coat,
  Where nae coat should be.

O how cam' this coat here?
  How can this be?
How cam' this coat here
  Without the leave o' me?

    A coat! quo' she:
    Ay, a coat, quo' he.
Ye auld blind dotard carl,
  Blind mat ye be,

It's but a pair of blankets
  My minnie sent to me.

  ··Blankets! quo' he:
    Ay, blankets, quo' she.
Far hae I ridden,
  And muckle hae I seen,
But buttons upon blankets
  Saw I never nane.

Ben gaed our gudeman,
  And ben gaed he;
And there he spied a sturdy man,
  Where nae man should be.

How cam' this man here?
  How can this be?
How cam' this man here,
  Without the leave o' me?

  A man! quo' she:
    Ay, a man, quo' he.
Poor blind body,
  And blinder mat ye be,
It's a new milking maid,
  My mither sent to me.

  A maid! quo' he:
    Ay, a maid, quo' she.
Far hae I ridden,
  And muckle hae I seen,
But lang-bearded maidens
  "Saw I" never nane.

SONG XXIII.*

WHAT CAN A YOUNG LASSIE DO WI' AN AULD MAN.

BY ROBERT BURNS.

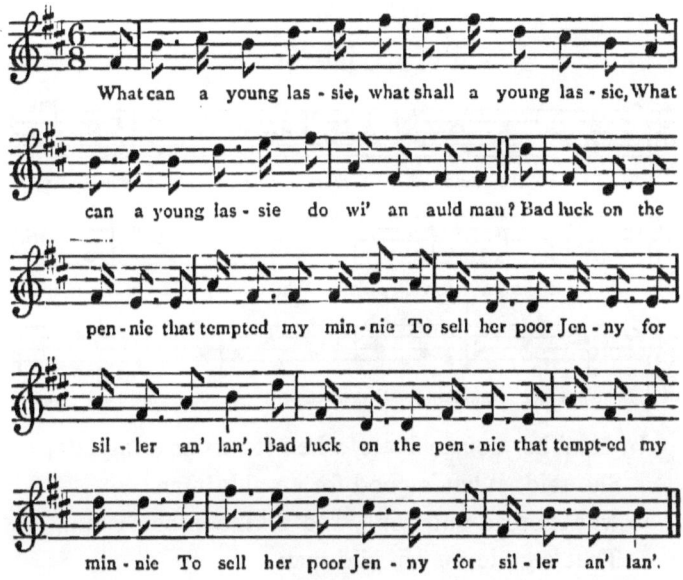

What can a young las-sie, what shall a young las-sie, What can a young las-sie do wi' an auld man? Bad luck on the pen-nie that tempted my min-nie To sell her poor Jen-ny for sil-ler an' lan', Bad luck on the pen-nie that tempt-ed my min-nie To sell her poor Jen-ny for sil-ler an' lan'.

He's always compleenin' frae morning to e'enin',
    He hosts and he hirples the weary day lang;
He's doyl't and he's dozin, his blude it is frozen:
    O, dreary's the night wi' a crazy auld man!

He hums and he hankers, he frets and he cankers,
    I never can please him, do a' that I can;
He's peevish, and jealous of a' the young fellows:
    O, dool on the day I met wi' an auld man!

My auld auntie Katie upon me taks pity,
  I'll do my endeavour to follow her plan;
I'll cross him, and wrack him, until I heart break him,
  And then his auld brass will buy me a new pan.

SONG XXIV.

MY AULD MAN.

In the land of Fife there lived a wick-ed wife, And in the town of Cu-par then, Who sore-ly did la-ment, and made her com-plaint, Oh when will ye dee, my auld man?

In cam' her cousin Kate, when it was growing late,
  She said, What's good for an auld man?
O wheat-bread and wine, and a kinnen new slain,
  That's gude for an auld man.

Cam' ye in to jeer, or cam' you to scorn,
  Or what cam' you for in?
For "bear"-bread and water, I'm sure is much better,
  It's o'er gude for an auld man.

Now the auld man's dead, and without remead,
  Into his cauld grave he is gane;
Lie still, wi' my blessing, of thee I hae nae missing,
  I'll ne'er mourn for an auld man.

Within a little mair then three quarters of a year,
    She was married to a young man then,
Who drank at the wine, and tippled at the beer,
    And spent mair gear than he wan.

O black grew her brows, and howe grew her een,
    And cauld grew her pat and her pan:
And now she sighs, and aye she says,
    I wish I had my silly auld man.

SONG XXV.

My fa-ther has for-ty gude shil-lings, Ha! ha! gude shil-lings! And nev-er had daugh-ter but me; My mo-ther she is right wil-ling, Ha! ha! right wil-ling! That I shall hae a' when they dee. And I won-der when I'll be mar-ried, Ha! ha! be mar-ried! My beau-ty be-gins to de-cay: It's time to

catch haud o' some-bo-dy, Ha! ha! some-bo-dy! Be-fore it

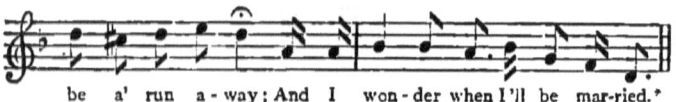
be a' run a-way; And I won-der when I'll be mar-ried.*

  My shoon they are at the mending,
   My buckles they are in the chest;
  My stockings are ready for sending:
   Then I'll be as braw as the rest.
  And I wonder, &c.

* The correction *it*, instead of *they*, the reading of the original, is from an old English ballad, in the black letter, entitled, "The Maiden's sad complaint for want of a Husband. To the New West Countrey tune; or, Hogh, when shall I be married? By L. W," (a misprint, as it should seem, for J. W., *i.e.*, John Wade,) the first, second, and fifth stanzas whereof (for there are fourteen in all) are either taken from, or have given rise to the present song. The reader shall judge for himself.

   "O when shall I be married,
    Hogh be married?
   My beauty begins to decay:
   'Tis time to find out somebody,
    Hogh somebody,
   Before it is quite gone away.

   "My father hath forty good shillings,
    Hogh good shillings,
   And never had daughter but me:
   My mother is also willing,
    Hogh so willing,
   That I shall have all if she die.

   "My mother she gave me a ladle,
    Hogh a ladle,'
   And that for the present lies by:
   My aunt she hath promist a cradle,
    Hogh a cradle,
   When any man with me does lie."

My father will buy me a ladle,
　At my wedding we'll hae a good sang;
For my uncle will buy me a cradle,
　To rock my child in when it's young.
And I wonder, &c.

SONG XXVI.

SLIGHTED NANSY.

To the Tune of "An the Kirk wad let me be."

It's I hae seven braw new gowns, And i-ther seven bet-ter to mak, And yet for a' my new gowns, My woo-er has turn'd his back. Be-sides, I hae sev-en milk kye, And San-dy he has but three; And yet for a' my good kye, The lad-die win-na hae me.

My daddie's a delver of dykes,
　My mither can card and spin,
And I am a fine fodgel lass,
　And the siller comes linkin' in:

U

The siller comes linkin' in,
   And it is fu' fair to see,
And fifty times wow! O wow!
   What ails the lads at me?

Whenever our Bawty does bark,
   Then fast to the door I rin,
To see gin ony young spark
   Will light and venture but in:
But never a ane will come in,
   Tho' mony a ane gaes by,
Syne far ben the house I rin,
   And a weary wight am I.

When I was at my first prayers,
   I pray'd but ane i' the year,
I wish'd for a handsome young lad,
   And a lad wi' muckle gear.
When I was at my neist prayers,
   I pray'd but now and than,
I fash'd na my head about gear,
   If I gat a handsome young man.

Now when I'm at my last prayers,
   I pray on baith night and day,
And O! if a beggar wad come,
   With that same beggar I'd gae.
And O! and what'll come o' me?
   And O! and what'll I do?
That sic a braw lassie as I
   Should die for a wooer I trow!*

* In the "Orpheus Caledonius," where the first, fourth, and fifth

SONG XXVII.

WHAT AILS THE LASSES AT ME.

To the Tune, "An the Kirk wad let me be." *

BY ALEXANDER ROSS,
SCHOOLMASTER AT LOCHLEE.

I AM a batchelor winsome,
    A farmer by rank and degree,
An' few I see gang out mair handsome,
    To kirk or to market than me;
I have outsight and insight and credit,
    And from any eelift I'm free,
I'm well enough boarded and bedded,
    And what ails the lasses at me?

My bughts of good store are no scanty,
    My byres are well stockèd wi' kye,
Of meal i' my girnels is plenty,
    An' twa or three easements forby.

of the above stanzas are entirely omitted, the last verse is as follows:—

    "I had an auld wife to my minny,
        And wow gin she kept me lang,
    And now the carlin's dead,
        And I'll do what I can.
    And I'll do what I can,
        Wi' my twenty pound and my cow;
    But wow it's an unco thing
        That naebody comes to wooe."

* See before, p. 305.

A horse to ride out when they're weary,
   An' cock with the best they can see,
An' then be ca'd dawty and deary,
   I fairely what ails them at me.

Behind backs, afore fouk I've woo'd them,
   An' a' the gates o't that I ken,
An' when they leugh on me, I trow'd them,
   An' thought I had won—but what then?
When I speak of matters they grumble,
   Nor are condescending and free,
But at my proposals aye stumble—
   I wonder what ails them at me.

I've tried them baith Highland and Lowland,
   Where I a good bargain could see,
But nane o' them fand I wad fall in,
   Or say they wad buckle wi' me.
With jooks an' wi' scrapes I've address'd them,
   Been with them baith modest and free,
But whatever way I caress'd them,
   There's something still ails them at me.

Oh, if I kenn'd how but to gain them,
   How fond of the knack wad I be!
Or what an address could obtain them,
   It should be twice welcome to me.
If kissing an' clapping wad please them,
   That trade I should drive till I die;
But, however I study to ease them,
   They've still an exception at me.

There's wratacks, an' cripples, an' cranshaks,
    An' a' the wandoghts that I ken,
No sooner they speak to the wenches,
    But they are ta'en far enough ben;
But when I speak to them that's stately,
    I find them aye ta'en wi' the gee,
An' get the denial right flatly;
    What, think ye, can ail them at me?

I have yet but ae offer to mak' them,
    If they wad but hearken to me,
And that is, I'm willing to tak them,
    If they their consent wad but gie;
Let her that's content write a billet,
    An' get it transmitted to me,
I hereby engage to fulfil it,
    Tho' cripple, tho' blind she sud be.

BILLET BY JEANY GRADDEN.

BY ALEXANDER ROSS.

DEAR batchelor, I've read your billet,
    Your strait an' your hardships I see,
An' tell you it shall be fulfilled,
    Tho' it were by none ither but me.
These forty years I've been neglected,
    An' nane has had pity on me;
Such offers should not be rejected,
    Whoever the offerer be.

For beauty I lay no claim to it,
    Or, may be, I had been away;
Tho' tocher or kindred could do it,
    I have no pretensions to thae:
The most I can say, I'm a woman,
    An' that I a wife want to be;
An' I'll tak exception at no man,
    That's willing to tak nane at me.

And now I think I may be cocky,
    Since fortune has smurtled on me,
I'm Jenny, and ye shall be Jockie,
    'Tis right we together sud be;
For nane of us cud find a marrow,
    So sadly forfairn were we;
Fouk sud no at anything tarrow,
    Whose chance look'd naething to be.

On Tuesday speer for Jeany Gradden,
    When I in my pens mean to be,
Just at the sign of the Old Maiden,
    Where ye shall be sure to meet me:
Bring with you the priest for the wedding,
    That a' things just ended may be,
An' we'll close the whole with the bedding;
    An' wha'll be sae merry as we?

A cripple I'm not, ye forsta' me,
    Tho' lame of a hand that I be;
Nor blind is there reason to ca' me,
    Altho' I see but with ae ee:

But I'm just the chap that you wanted,
  So tightly our state doth agree;
For nane wad hae you, ye have granted,
  As few I confess wad hae me.

———◆———

SONG XXVIII.

OF all the things beneath the sun,
  To love's the greatest curse;
If one's denied, then he's undone,
  If not, 'tis ten times worse.
Poor Adam, by his wife, 'tis known,
  Was trick'd some years ago;
But Adam was not trick'd alone,
  For all his sons were so.

Lovers the strangest fools are made,
  When they their nymphs pursue;
Which they will ne'er believe, till wed,
  But then, alas! 'tis true.
They beg, they pray, and they adore,
  Till wearied out of life;
And pray what's all this trouble for?
  Why, truly, for a wife.

How odd a thing's a whining sot,
  Who sighs, in greatest need,
For that which, soon as ever got,
  Does make him sigh indeed.

Each maid's an angel while she's woo'd,
   But when the wooing's done,
The wife, instead of flesh and blood,
   Proves nothing but a bone.

Ills, more or less, in human life,
   No mortal man can shun;
But when a man has got a wife,
   He has them all in one.
The liver of Prometheus
   A gnawing vulture fed;
A fable,—but the thing was thus,
   The poor old man was wed.

A wife, all men of learning know,
   Was Tantalus's curse;
The apples which did tempt him so,
   Were nought but a divorce.
Let no fool dream, that to his share
   A better wife will fall;
They're all the same, faith, to a hair,
   For they are women all.

When first the senseless empty nokes
   With wooing does begin,
Far better he might beg the stocks,
   That they would let him in.
Yet for a lover, we may say,
   He wears no cheating phiz;
Tho' others' looks do oft betray,
   He looks like what he is.

More joys a glass of wine does give,
 (Wife take him that gainsays,)
Than all the wenches sprung from Eve
 E'er gave in all their days.
Then come, to lovers here's a glass;
 God wot they need no curse;
Each wishes he may wed his lass,
 No soul can wish him worse.

SONG XXIX.

OF EVILL WYFFIS.

BY —— FLEMYNG.*

BE mirry, bretherene, ane and all,
 And sett all sturt on syd;
And every ane togidder call,
 To God to be our gyd:
For als lang leivis the mirry man,
As dois the wrech, for ocht he can;
Quhen Deid him streks, he wait nocht quhan,
 And chairgis him to byd.

---

* Written before 1568. "Every reader," Lord Hailes observes, "will perceive a want of connexion in this poem. The first and second stanzas contain moral reflections on the certainty of death; the third is a religious inference; the fourth mentions the dangers attending the profession of a sailor; the fifth insensibly slides into an invective on froward wives; and this subject is carried on through the rest of the poem, with some wit and much acrimony of expression."

The riche than sall nocht sparit be,
    Thocht thay haif gold and land,
Nor zit the fair, for thair bewty,
    Can nocht that chairge ganestand :
Thocht wicht or waik wald fle away,
No dowt bot all mon ransone pay;
Quhat place, or quhair, can no man say,
    Be sie, or zit be land.

Quhairfoir, my counsaill, brethir, is,
    That we togidder sing,
And all to loif that lord of bliss,
    That is of hevynis king :
Quha knawis the secreit thochts and dowt,
Off all our hairtis round about;
And he quha thinkis him nevir sa stout,
    Mone thoill that punissing.

Quhat man but stryf, in all his lyfe,
    Doith test moir of deidis pane,
Nor dois the man quhilk on the sie
    His leving seikis to gane :
For quhen distress dois him oppress,
Than to the lord for his redress,
Quha gaif command for all express
    To call, and nocht refrane.

The myrryest man that leivis on lyfe,
    He sailis on the sie;
For he knawis nowdir sturt nor stryfe,
    Bot blyth and mirry be :

Bot he that hes ane evill wyfe,
Hes sturt and sorrow all his lyfe :
And that man quhilk leivis ay in stryfe,
   How can he mirry be ?

Ane evill wyfe is the werst aucht
   That ony man can haif ;
For he may nevir sit in saucht,
   Onless he be hir sklaif :
Bot of that sort I knaw nane uder,
But owthir a kukald, or his bruder ;
"Fondlars" and kukkaldis all togider,
   May wiss thair wyfis in graif.

Becauss thair wyfis hes maistery,
   That thay dar nawayiss cheip,
Bot gif it be in privity,
   Quhan thair wyfis ar on sleip :
Ane mirry in thair cumpany
Wer to thame baith gold and fy ;
Ane menstrall could nocht bocht be,
   Thair mirth gif he could beit.*

Bot of that sort quhilk I report,
   I knaw nane in this ring ;
Bot we may all, baith grit and small,
   Glaidly baith dance and sing :

---

* "The meaning is, to such hen-pecked husbands a cheerful companion would be a most valuable acquisition. A musician that could keep them in tune would be worth any money."—Lord HAILES.

Quha list nocht heir to mak gud cheir,
Perchance his gudis ane uthir zeir
Be spent, quhen he is brocht to beir,
    Quhen his wyfe takis the fling.

It has bene sene, that wyse wemen,
    Eftir thair husbandis deid,
Hes gottin men hes gart thame ken
    Gif thay mycht beir grit laid.
With ane grene sting,* hes gart thame bring
The geir quhilk won wes be ane dring;
And syne gart all the bairnis sing
    Ramukloch in thair "bed."

Than wad scho say, Allace! this day,
    For him that wan this geir;
Quhen I him had, I skairsly said,
    My hairt, anis mak gud cheir.
Or I had lettin him spend a plak,
I lever haif wittin him brokin his bak,
Or ellis his craig had gottin a crak,
    Our the heicht of the stair.

---

* A sting is "a slender hazel stick new cut, for the purpose of giving moderate correction to a wife. This was a power which our rude legislature in former times committed to husbands."—Lord HAILES. In England, at least, it is still good law, and has been lately declared so from the Bench,—provided, however, the implement of correction exceed not the thickness of the Judge's thumb, of which all husbands are presumed to have the exact measure: *Ignorantia legis non excusat.*

Ye neigartis, then example tak,
  And leir to spend zour awin;
And with gud freyndis ay mirry mak,
  That it may be weill knawin,
That thow art he quha wan this geir;
And for thy wyfe se thou nocht spair,
With gud freyndis ay to mak repair,
  Thy honesty may be "shawin."

Finis, quod I, quha settis nocht by
  The ill wyffis of this toun,
Thocht for dispyt with me wald flyt,
  Gif thay micht put me doun.
Gif ze wald knaw quha maid this sang,
Quhidder ze will him heid or hang,
Flemyng is his name, quhair evir he gang,
  In place, or in quhat toun.

SONG XXX.

THE BLATHRIE O'T.

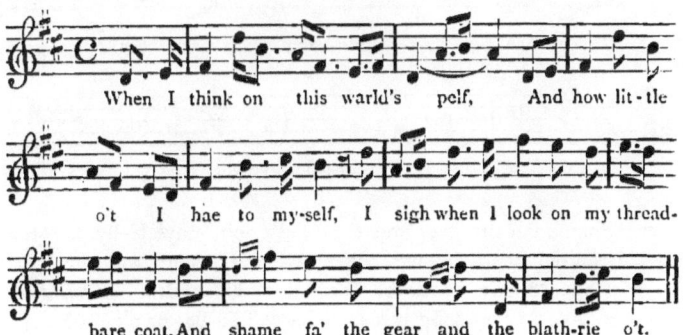

When I think on this warld's pelf, And how little o't I hae to my-self, I sigh when I look on my thread-bare coat, And shame fa' the gear and the blath-rie o't.

Johnnie was the lad that held the pleuch,
But now he has got goud and gear eneuch;
I weel mind the day when he wasna worth a groat,
And shame fa' the gear and the blathrie o't.

Jenny was the lassie that mucked the byre,
But now she goes in her silken attire:
And she was a lass who wore a plaiden coat,
And shame fa' the gear and the blathrie o't.

Yet a' this shall never daunton me,
Sae lang's I keep my fancy free;
While I've but a penny to pay the tither pot,
May the d—l take the gear and the blathrie o't.*

SONG XXXI.

TODLIN' BUTT AND TODLIN' BEN.

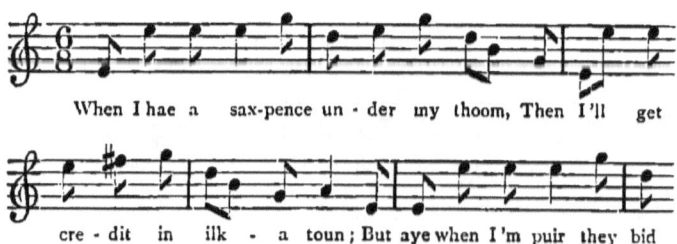

When I hae a sax-pence un-der my thoom, Then I'll get
cre-dit in ilk-a toun; But aye when I'm puir they bid

---

* "Shame fall the geer and the blad'ry o't," says Kelly, is "the turn of an old Scottish song, spoken when a young handsome girl marries an old man upon the account of his wealth."—*Scots Proverbs*, p. 296. [This song is also called " The Bagrie o't."—ED.]

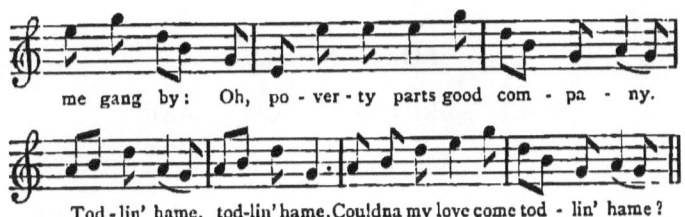

me gang by: Oh, po-ver-ty parts good com-pa-ny. Tod-lin' hame, tod-lin' hame, Couldna my love come tod-lin' hame?

Fair-fa' the gudewife, and send her gude sale,
She gies us white bannocks to relish her ale,
Syne if that her tippeny chance to be sma',
We'll take a good scour o't, and ca't awa'.
    Todlin' hame, todlin' hame,
    As round as a neep come todlin' hame.

My kimmer and I lay down to sleep,
Wi' twa pint-stoups at our bed's feet;
And aye when we waken'd, we drank them dry:
What think ye of my wee kimmer and I?
    Todlin' butt, and todlin' ben,
    Sae round as my love comes todlin' hame.

Leeze me on liquor, my todlin' doo,
Ye're aye sae good humour'd when weeting your mou;
When sober sae sour, ye'll fight wi' a flee,
That 'tis a blythe sight to the bairns and me,
    When todlin' hame, todlin' hame,
    When round as a neep ye come todlin' hame.

SONG XXXII.

WILLIE BREW'D A PECK O' MAUT.

BY ROBERT BURNS.

He are we met, three merry boys,
Three merry boys I trow are we;
And mony a night we've merry been,
And mony mae we hope to be.
  We are na fou, &c.

It is the moon, I ken her horn,
    That's blinkin in the lift sae hie;
She shines sae bright to wyle us hame,
    But by my sooth she'll wait a wee.
        We are na fou, &c.

Wha first shall rise to gang awa,
    A cuckold coward loun is he;
Wha last beside his chair shall fa',
    He is the king amang us three.
        We are na fou, &c.

SONG XXXIII.

BALLAT OF GUDE-FALLOWIS.*

I mak it kend, he that will spend,
    And luve God lait and air,
God will him mend, and grace him send,
    Quhen catyvis sall haif cair:
Thairfoir pretend weill for to spend
    Off geir, and nocht till spair.
I knaw the end, that all mon wend
    Away nakit and bair,
With ane O and ane I;
    Ane wreche sall haif no mair,
Bot ane schort scheit, at heid and feit,
    For all his wrek and wair.

---

* Written before 1568. The name of Johne Blyth, subjoined in the original MS., seems to have been only assumed for the occasion.

For all the wrak a wreche can pak,
    And in his baggis imbrace,
Zit Deid sall tak him be the bak,
    And gar him cry, Allace!
Than sall he swak away with lak,
    And wait nocht to quhat place;
Than will thay mak at him a knak,
    That maist of his gud hais,
    With ane O and ane I:
    Quhyle we haif tyme and space,
Mak we gud cheir, quhyle we "are" heir,
    And thank God of his grace.

Wer thair ane king to rax and ring
    Amang gude fallowis cround,
Wrechis wald wring, and mak murnyng,
    For dule thay suld be dround;
Quha findis ane dring, owdir auld or zing,
    Gar hoy him out and hound.
Now let us sing, with Chrystis blissing,
    Be glaid, and mak gud sound,
    With ane O and ane I;
    Now, or we forder found,
Drink thow to me, and I to the,
    And lat the cop go round.

Quha undirstude, suld haife his gude,
    Or he wer closd in clay,
Sum in thair mude they wald go wud,
    And de lang or thair day:

Nocht worth ane hude, or ane auld snud,
Thow fall beir hyne away;
Wreche, be the rude, for to conclude,
Full few will for the pray,
With ane O and ane I:
Gud-fallowis, quhill we may,
Be mirry and free, syne blyth we be,
And sing on twa and tway.

SONG XXXIV.*

Care, a-way go thou from me, For I am not fit match for thee; Thou be-reaves me of my wits, Wherefore I hate thy fran-tic fits: Therefore I will care no more, Since that in cares comes no re-store; But I will sing, Hey down, a down, a dee, And cast care a-way, a-way from me.

Written before 1666.

If I want, I care to get;
The more I have, it doth me fret;
Have I much, I care for more;
The more I have, I think I'm poor:
Thus doth grief my mind oppress,
In wealth or wo finds no redress:
Therefore I'll care no more, no more in vain,
For care hath cost me mickle grief and pain.

Is not this world a slippery ball?
And thinks men strange to catch a fall.
Doth not the sea both ebb and flow?
And hath not fortune a painted show?
Why should men take care or grief,
Since that in care comes no relief?
There's none so wise but he may be o'erthrown,
The careless may reap what the careful hath sown.

Well then, learn to know thyself,
And care not for this worldly pelf:
Whether thine estate be great or small,
Give thanks to God, what e'er befall:
So shalt thou then live at ease,
No sudden grief shall thee displease:
Then may'st thou sing, Hey down, a down, a dee,
When thou hast cast all care and grief from thee.

SONG XXXV.

MAGGIE LAUDER.

BY FRANCIS SEMPLE OF BELTREES.

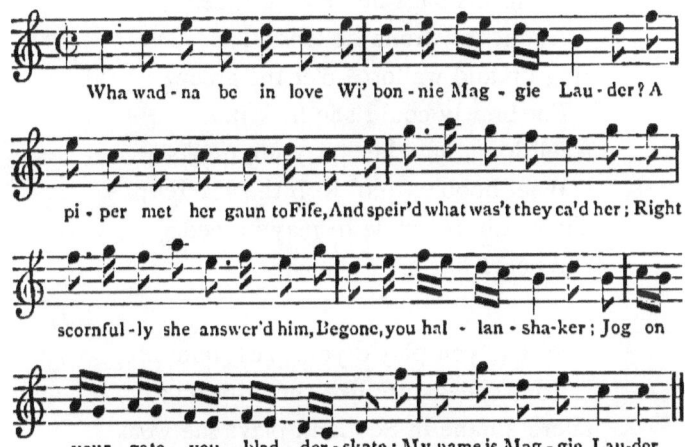

Wha wad-na be in love Wi' bon-nie Mag-gie Lau-der? A pi-per met her gaun to Fife, And speir'd what was't they ca'd her; Right scornful-ly she answer'd him, Begone, you hal-lan-sha-ker; Jog on your gate, you blad-der-skate; My name is Mag-gie Lau-der.

Maggie, quo' he, and, by my bags,
    I 'm fidging fain to see thee ;
Sit down by me, my bonnie bird,
    In troth I winna steer thee ;
For I 'm a piper to my trade,
    My name is Rob the Ranter,
The lasses loup as they were daft,
    When I blaw up my chanter.

Piper, quo' Meg, hae ye your bags ?
    Or is your drone in order ?
If you be Rob, I 've heard of you,
    Live you upo' the Border ?

The lasses a', baith far and near,
    Have heard of Rob the Ranter;
I 'll shake my foot wi' right goodwill,
    Gif you 'll blaw up your chanter.

Then to his bags he flew wi' speed,
    About the drone he twisted;
Meg up and wallop'd o'er the green,
    For brawly could she frisk it.
Weel done, quo' he: play up, quo' she:
    Weel bobb'd, quo' Rob the Ranter;
'Tis worth my while to play indeed,
    When I hae sic a dancer.

Weel hae you play'd your part, quo' Meg,
    Your cheeks are like the crimson;
There 's nane in Scotland plays sae weel,
    Since we lost Habbie Simpson.*
I 've lived in Fife, baith maid and wife,
    These ten years and a quarter;
Gin you should come to Anster fair,
    Speir ye for Maggie Lauder.

---

* The celebrated piper of Kilbarchan; whose memory and merits are preserved in an excellent elegy. He flourished about the middle of the seventeenth century.

SONG XXXVI.

ANDRO AND HIS CUTTY GUN.

Blythe, blythe and mer-ry was she, Blythe was she but and ben; And well she lo'ed a Haw-ick gill, And leugh to see a tap-pit hen. She took me in, and set me down, And heght to keep me law-ing free; But, cun-ning car-line that she was, She gart me birl my baw-bee.

We lo'ed the liquor well enough;
    But waes my heart my cash was done.
Before that I had quench'd my drouth,
    And laith I was to pawn my shoon.
When we had three times toom'd our stoup,
    And the niest chappin new begun,
Wha started in to heeze up our hope,
    But Andro wi' his cutty gun.

The carline brought her kebbuck ben,
   With girdle-cakes weel toasted broun,
Well does the canny kimmer ken,
   They gar the swats gae glibber down.
We ca'd the bicker aft about;
   Till dawning we ne'er jee'd our bun,
And aye the cleanest drinker out,
   Was Andro wi' his cutty gun.

He did like ony mavis sing,
   And as I in his oxter sat,
He ca'd me aye his bonnie thing,
   And mony a sappy kiss I gat.
I hae been east, I hae been west,
   I hae been far ayont the sun;
But the blythest lad that e'er I saw,
   Was Andro wi' his cutty gun.

SONG XXXVII.

WILLIE WAS A WANTON WAG.

BY WILLIAM WALKINSHAW OF WALKINSHAW.

Wil-lie was a wan-ton wag, The blyth-est lad that e'er I saw; At bri-dals still he bore the brag, And

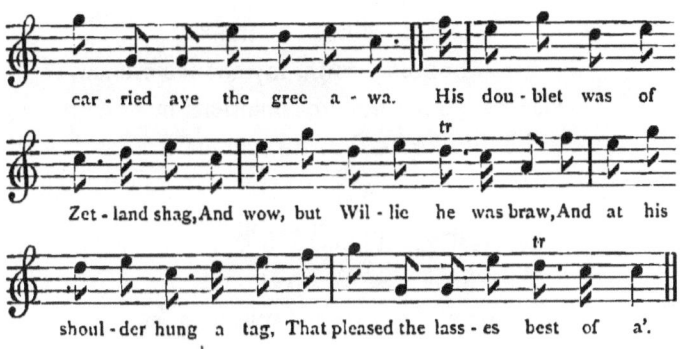

He was a man without a clag,
    His heart was frank without a flaw;
And aye whatever Willie said,
    It was still hauden as a law.
His boots they were made of the jag;
    When he went to the weaponshaw,
Upon the green nane durst him brag,
    The feind a ane amang them a'.

And wasna Willie weel worth gowd?
    He wan the love of great and sma';
For after he the bride had kiss'd,
    He kiss'd the lasses hale-sale a':
Sae merrily round the ring they row'd,
    When by the hand he led them a',
And smack on smack on them bestow'd,
    By virtue of a standing law.

And wasna Willie a great loun,
    As shyre a lick as e'er was seen?
When he danced wi' the lasses round,
    The bridegroom speer'd where he had been.

Quo' Willie, I've been at the ring,
    With bobbing, faith, my shanks are sair;
Gae ca' your bride and maidens in,
    For Willie he dow do nae mair.

Then rest ye, Willie; I'll gae out,
    And for a wee fill up the ring:
But, shame light on his souple snout,
    He wanted Willie's wanton fling.
Then straight he to the bride did fare,
    Says, Weel's me on your bonnie face,
With bobbing Willie's shanks are sair,
    And I am come to fill his place.

Bridegroom, she says, you'll spoil the dance,
    And at the ring you'll aye be lag,
Unless like Willie ye advance;
    O! Willie has a wanton leg:
For wi't he learns us a' to steer,
    And foremost aye bears up the ring;
We will find nae sic dancing here,
    If we want Willie's wanton fling.

SONG XXXVIII.

THE AULD WIFE AYONT THE FIRE.

There was a wife wonn'd in a glen, And she had dochters nine or ten, That sought the house baith but and ben, To find their mam a sneesh-in'. The auld wife a-yont the fire, The auld wife a-niest the fire, The auld wife a-boon the fire, She dee'd for lack o' sneesh-in'.

Her mill into some hole had fawn,
What recks, quo' she, let it be gawn,
For I maun hae a young gudeman,
   Shall furnish me with sneeshin'.
     The auld wife, &c.

Her eldest dochter said right bauld,
Fy, mother, mind that now ye 're auld,
And if ye with a yonker wald,
   He 'll waste awa your sneeshin'.
     The auld wife, &c.

The youngest dochter ga'e a shout,
O mother dear! your teeth's a' out,
Besides hauf-blind, you have the gout,
   Your mill can haud nae sneeshin'.
     The auld wife, &c.

Ye lee'd, ye limmers, cries auld mump,
For I hae baith a tooth and stump,
And will nae langer live in dump,
   By wantin' o' my sneeshin'.
     The auld wife, &c.

Thole ye, says Peg, that pawky slut,
Mother, if you can crack a nut,
Then we will a' consent to it,
   That you shall have a sneeshin'.
     The auld wife, &c.

The auld ane did agree to that,
And they a pistol bullet gat;
She powerfully began to crack,
   To won hersel' a sneeshin'.
     The auld wife, &c.

Braw sport it was to see her chow't,
An 'tween her gums sae squeeze and row't,
While frae her jaws the slaver flow'd,
   And aye she cursed poor stumpy.
     The auld wife, &c.

At last she saw a desperate squeeze,
Which brak the lang tooth by the neez,
And syne poor stumpy was at ease,
   But she tint hopes o' sneeshin'.
     The auld wife, &c.

She of the task began to tire,
And frae her dochters did retire,
Syne lean'd her down ayont the fire,
   And dee'd for lack o' sneeshin'.
     The auld wife, &c.

Ye auld wives, notice weel this truth,
As soon as ye're past mark of mouth,
Ne'er do what's only fit for youth,
   And leave aff thoughts o' sneeshin :
     Else, like this wife " ayont" the fire,
     Your bairns against you will conspire ;
     Nor will you get, unless ye hire,
     A young man with your sneeshin'.

SONG XXXIX.

THE ROCK AND THE WEE PICKLE TOW.

BY ALEXANDER ROSS,

SCHOOLMASTER AT LOCHLEE.

I 've wanted a sark for these eight years an' ten,
   An' this was to be the beginning o't,
But I vow I shall want it for as lang again,
   Or ever I try the spinning o't;

For never since ever they ca'd me as they ca' me,
Did sick a mishap an misanter befa' me,
But ye shall hae leave baith to hang me an' draw me,
    The neist time I try the spinning o't.

I hae keeped my house for these threescore o' years,
    An' aye I kept free o' the spinning o't,
But how I was sarked foul fa' them that speers,
    For it minds me upo' the beginning o't.
But our women are now-a-days grown sae braw,
That ilk ane maun hae a sark an' some hae twa,
The warld was better when ne'er ane ava'
    Had a rag but ane at the beginning o't.

Foul fa' her that ever advised me to spin,
    That had been sae lang a beginning o't,
I might well have ended as I did begin,
    Nor have got sic a skair with the spinning o't.
But they'll say, she's a wise wife that kens her ain weird,
I thought on a day, it should never be speer'd,
How lout ye the low take your rock by the beard,
    When ye yeed to try the spinning o't?

The spinning, the spinning it gars my heart sob,
    When I think upo' the beginning o't,
I thought ere I died to have anes made a wob,
    But still I had weers o' the spinning o't.
But had I nine dothers, as I hae but three,
The safest and soundest advice I could gie,
Is that they frae spinning wad keep their hands free,
    For fear of a bad beginning o't.

Yet in spite of my counsel if they will needs run
    The drearysome risk of the spinning o't,
Let them seek out a lyth in the heat of the sun,
    And there venture on the beginning o't:
But to do as I did, alas, and awow!
To busk up a rock at the cheek of the low,
Says, that I had but little wit in my pow,
    And as little ado wi' the spinning o't.

But yet after a', there is ae thing that grieves
    My heart to think o' the beginning o't,
Had I won the length but of ae pair o' sleeves,
    Then there had been word o' the spinning o't;
This I wad ha' washen an' bleech'd like the snaw,
And o' my twa gardies like moggans wad draw,
An' then fouk wad say that auld Girzy was braw,
    An' a' was upon her ain spinning o't.

But gin I could shog about till a new spring,
    I should yet hae a bout of the spinning o't,
A mutchkin of linseed I'd i' the yerd fling,
    For a' the wanchancy beginning o't.
I'll gar my ain Tammie gae down to the how,
An' cut me a rock of a widdershins grow,
Of good rantry-tree for to carry my tow,
    An' a spindle o' same for the twining o't.

For now when I mind me, I met Maggie Grim,
    This morning just at the beginning o't,
She was never ca'd chancy, but canny an' slim,
    An' sae it has fared with my spinning o't:

But gin my new rock war anes cutted an' dry,
I'll a' Maggie's cann an' her cantrips defy,
An' but onie sussie the spinning I'll try,
   An' ye shall a' hear o' the beginning o't.

Quo' Tibby, her dother, tak tent fat ye say,
   The never a rag we'll be seeking o't,
Gin ye anes begin, ye'll tarveal's night an' day,
   Sae it's vain ony mair to be speaking o't.
Since Lammas I'm now gain' thirty an' twa,
An' never a dud sark had I yet gryt or sma',
An' what war am I? I'm as warm an' as braw
   As thrummy tail'd Meg, that's the spinner o't.

To labour the lint-land, an' then buy the seed,
   An' then to yoke me to the harrowing o't,
An' syne loll amon't an' pike out ilka weed,
   Like swine in a stye at the farrowing o't;
Syne powing an' ripling an' steeping, an' then
To gar's gae an' spread it upo' the cauld plain,
An' then after a' maybe labour in vain,
   When the wind and the weet gets the fusion o't.

But tho' it should anter the weather to byde,
   Wi' beetles we're set to the drubbing o't,
An' then frae our fingers to gnidge aff the hide,
   With the wearisome wark o' the rubbing o't.
An' syne ilka tait maun be heckled out throw,
The lint putten ae gate, anither the tow,
Syne on a rock wi't, an' it taks a low,
   The back o' my hand to the spinning o't.

Quo' Jenny, I think, 'oman, ye 're i' the right,
    Set your feet aye a spar to the spinning o't,
Let's tak an example frae our ain mither's fright,
    That she gat when she try'd the beginning o't.
But they 'll say that auld fouk are twice bairns indeed,
An' sae she has kyth'd it, but there is nae need
To sickan an amshach that we drive our head,
    As lang 's we 're sae skair'd frae the spinning o't.

Quo' Nanny the youngest, I 've now heard you a',
    An' dowie's your doom o' the spinning o't,
Gin ye, fan the cow flings, the cog cast awa',
    Ye 'll see where ye 'll lick up your winning o't.
But I see that, but spinning, I 'll never be braw,
But gae by the name of a dilp or a daw,
Sae lack, where ye like, I shall anes shak a fa',
    Afore I be dung with the spinning o't.

For well I can mind me when black Willie Bell
    Had Tibbie there just at the winning o't,
What blew up the bargain, she kens well hersel',
    Was the want o' the knack o' the spinning o't.
An' now, poor 'oman, for ought that I ken,
She may never get sic an offer again,
But pine awa' bit an' bit, like Jenkin's hen,
    An' naething to wyte but the spinning o't.

But were it for naething, but just this alane,
    I shall yet hae a bout o' the spinning o't,
They may cast me for ca'ing me black at the bane,
    But nae cause I shun the beginning o't.

But, be that as it happens, I care not a strae,
But nane of the lads shall e'er hae it to say,
When they come to woo, she kens naething avae,
    Nor has ony knack o' the spinning o't.

In the days they ca'd yore, gin auld fouks had but won,
    To a surcoat hough-side for the winning o't,
Of coat raips well cut by the cast o' their bun,
    They never sought mair o' the spinning o't.
A pair of grey hoggers well clinked benew,
Of nae other litt but the hue of the ewe,
With a pair of rough rullions to scuff thro' the dew,
    Was the fee they sought at the beginning o't.

But we maun hae linen, an' that maun hae we,
    An how get we that, but the spinning o't?
How can we hae face for to seek a gryt fee,
    Except we can help at the winning o't?
An' we maun hae pearlins and mabbies an cocks,
An' some other thing that the ladies ca' smocks,
An' how get we that, gin we tak nae our rocks,
    And rug what we can at the spinning o't?

'Tis needless for us for to tak our remarks
    Frae our mithers miscooking the spinning o't,
She never kent ought o' the gude o' the sarks,
    Frae this aback to the beginning o't.
Twa three ell o' plaiden was a' that was sought
By our auld warld bodies, an' that boot be bought,
For in ilka town sicken things was na wrought,
    So little they kent o' the spinning o't.

SONG XL.

TARRY WOO'.

Tar-ry woo', tar-ry woo', Tar-ry woo' is ill to spin, Card it weil, card it weil, Card it weil ere ye be-gin, When 'tis card-ed, row'd, and spun, Then the work is haf-lens done; But when wo-ven, dress'd, and clean, It may be clead-in' for a queen.

Sing my bonnie harmless sheep,
That feed upon the mountains steep,
Bleeting sweetly as ye go
Through the winter's frost and snow:
Hart and hynd, and fallow deer,
Not by half so useful are;
Frae kings to him that hauds the plow,
Are all oblig'd to tarry woo'.

Up ye shepherds, dance and skip,
O'er the hills and valleys trip;
Sing up the praise of tarry woo',
Sing the flocks that bear it too;
Harmless creatures without blame,
That clead the back, and cram the wame,
Keep us warm and hearty fou;
Leese me on the tarry woo'.

How happy is a shepherd's life,
Far frae courts, and free of strife!
While the gimmers bleet and bae,
And the lambkins answer mae;
No such music to his ear;
Of thief or fox he has no fear;
Sturdy kent, and collie true,
Weil defend the tarry woo'.

He lives content and envies none;
Not even a monarch on his throne,
Tho' he the royal sceptre sways,
Has not sweeter holidays.
Who'd be a king, can ony tell,
When a shepherd sings sae weil?
Sings sae weil, and pays his due,
With honest heart and tarry woo'.

SONG XLI.

THE EWIE WI' THE CROOKED HORN.

BY THE REV. JOHN SKINNER.

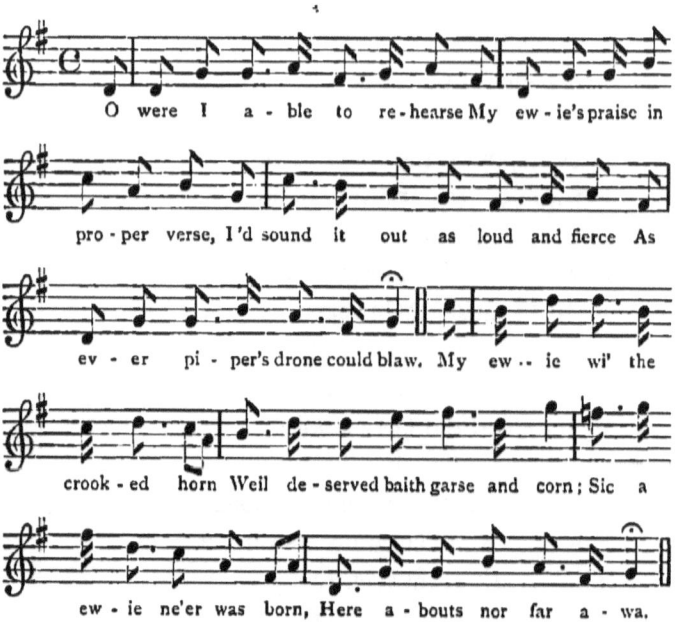

She neither needed tar nor keil,
To mark her upon hip or heel,
Her crooked horn it did as weil,
    To ken her by amang them a'.
    My ewie, &c.

She never threaten'd scab nor rot,
But keeped aye her ain jog trot,

Baith to the fauld and to the cot,
 Was never sweir to lead nor ca'.
  My ewie, &c.

Nae cauld nor hunger e'er her dang,
Nor win' nor rain could e'er her wrang,
For anes she lay a hale week lang
 Aneath a drearie wreath o' snaw.
  My ewie, &c.

When other ewies lap the dyke,
And ate the kail for a' the tyke,
My ewie never play'd the like,
 But tees'd about the barn yard wa'.
  My ewie, &c.

A better nor a thriftier beast
Nae honest man could well hae wist,
For, bonnie thing, she never mist
 To hae ilk year a lamb or twa.
  My ewie, &c.

The first she had I gae to Jock,
To be to him a kind o' stock,
And now the laddie has a flock
 O' mair nor thirty head to ca'.
  My ewie, &c.

The neist I gae to Jean; and now
The bairn's sae braw, has fauld sae fu',
That lads sae thick come her to woo,
 They're fain to sleep on hay or straw.
  My ewie, &c.

I looked aye at even for her,
For fear the fumart might devour her,
Or some mishanter should come o'er her,
    If the beastie bade awa'.
      My ewie, &c.

Yet last week, for a' my keeping,
I canna speak it without greeting,
A villain came, when I was sleeping,
    And sta' my ewie, horn and a'.
      My ewie, &c.

I sought her sair upon the morn;
And down aneath a buss o' thorn
I got my ewie's crooked horn,
    But ah! my ewie was awa'.
      My ewie, &c.

But gin I had the loon that did it,
I've sworn and bann'd, as weel as said it,
Tho' a' the world should forbid it,
    I shall gie his neck a thraw.
      My ewie, &c.

I never met wi' sic a turn
As this since ever I was born,
My ewie wi' the crooked horn,
    Puir silly ewie! stown awa'.
      My ewie, &c.

O! had she died o' croup or cauld,
As ewies die when they are auld,
It wad na been, by mony fauld,
  Sae sair a heart to nane o's a'.
  My ewie, &c.

For a' the claith that we ha'e worn,
Frae her and hers, sae aften shorn,
The loss o' her we could ha'e borne,
  Had fair strae death ta'en her awa'.
  My ewie, &c.

But this puir thing to lose her life,
Aneath a greedy villain's knife,
I'm really fear'd that our gudewife
  Shall never win aboon't ava.
  My ewie, &c.

O! a' ye bards benorth Kinghorn,
Call up your muses, let them mourn;
Our ewie wi' the crooked horn
  Is frae us stown, and fell'd and a'.
  My ewie, &c.

CLASS THE THIRD.

SONG I.

FLODDEN HILL; OR, FLOWERS OF THE FOREST.*

BY MISS JANE ELLIOT OF MINTO.

I've heard them lilt-in' at the ewes' milk-in',
Lass-es a-lilt-in' be-fore dawn o' day;
But now there's a moan-in' on ilk-a green loan-in',
That our braw for-est-ers are a' wede a-way.

* The battle of Flodden, or, as the English usually call it, Flodden-field, of which the mournful effects are so pathetically described in these beautiful stanzas, was fought the 9th day of September 1513, between James IV., King of Scots, and Thomas Howard,

At bughts in the mornin', nae blythe lads are scornin',
Lasses are lanely, and dowie, and wae;
Nae daffin, nae gabbin, but sighin', and sabbin';
Ilk ane lifts her leglin, and hies her away.

At e'en in the gloamin', nae swankies are roamin',
'Bout stacks wi' the lasses, at bogle to play;
But ilk maid sits drearie, lamentin' her dearie,
The flowers of the forest, that are wede away.

In ha'rst at the shearin', nae youths now are jeerin',
Bandsters are runkled, and lyart, or grey;
At fair or at preachin', nae wooin', nae fleechin',
Since our braw foresters are now wede away.

Dool for the order, sent our lads to the Border,
The English for ance by guile wan the day;
The flowers of the forest, that aye shone the foremost,
The prime of our land, lie cauld in the clay.

We'll hear nae mair liltin', at our ewes milkin',
Women and bairns are heartless and wae;
Sighin' and moanin' on ilka green loanin',
The flowers of the forest are a' wede away.

Earl of Surrey, that gallant monarch, with most of his nobility, and the greater part of his army, composed of the flower of the Scotish youth, being left dead on the field.

Flodden is a hill or eminence in Northumberland, upon which the Scots encamped previous to the battle: for an account of which, see Buchanan, Lindsay, Drummond, and the common English and Scotish histories.

SONG II.

SIR PATRICK SPENCE.*

The king sits in Dum-fer-ling toune, Drink-ing the blude-reid wine: O quhar will I get a guid sail-or, To sail this schip of mine?

Up an spak an eldern knicht,
    Sat at the king's richt kne:
Sir Patrick Spence is the best sailor
    That sails upon the se.

The king has written a braid letter,
    And sign'd it wi' his hand;
And sent it to Sir Patrick Spence,
    Was walking on the sand.

The first line that Sir Patrick red,
    A loud lauch lauchèd he;
The next line that Sir Patrick red,
    The teir blinded his ee.

* No memorial of the subject of this ballad occurs in history; but it apparently belongs to the present class, and probably to this period.

O quha is this has don this deid,
    This ill deid don to me;
To send me out this time o' the zeir,
    To sail upon the se?

Mak haste, mak haste, my mirry men all,
    Our guid schip sails the morne.
O say na sae, my master deir,
    For I feir a deadlie storme.

Late, late yestreen I saw the new moone,
    Wi' the auld moone in hir arme;
And I feir, I feir, my deir master,
    That we will com to harme.

O our Scots nobles wer richt laith
    To weet their cork-heild schoone;
Bot lang owre a' the play wer play'd,
    Thair hats they swam aboone.

O lang, lang may thair ladies sit
    Wi' their fans into thair hand,
Or eir they se Sir Patrick Spence
    Cum sailing to the land.

O lang, lang may the ladies stand,
    Wi' thair gold kems in thair hair,
Waiting for thair ain deir lords,
    For they'll se thame na mair.

SCOTISH SONGS.

Have owre, have owre to Aberdour,*
It's fiftie fadom deip:
And thair lies guid Sir Patrick Spence,
Wi' the Scots lords at his feit.

SONG III.

JOHNIE ARMSTRANG.†

Sum speiks of lords, sum speiks of lairds, And sic-lyke men of hie de-grie; Of a

---

* "A village lying upon the river Forth, the entrance to which is sometimes denominated *De mortuo mari.*"—*Percy.*

† "The king [*i.e.,* James V.] . . . . gart set a parliament at Edinburgh, the twenty-eighth day of March, one thousand five hundred and twenty-eight years, and . . . . syne after, made a convention at Edinburgh, with all his whole lords and barons, to consult how he might stanch all theft and reving within his realm, and cause the commons to live in peace, which long time had been perturbed before, for fault of good guiding of an old king. To this effect, the king made proclamations to all lords, barons, gentlemen, landward men, and freeholders, that they should compear at Edinburgh, with a month's victual, to pass with the king where he pleased, to danton the thieves of Teviotdale, Anandale, Liddisdale, and other parts of that country; and also warned all gentlemen that had good dogs to bring them, that he might hunt in the said country as he pleased.

"The second day of June the king past out of Edinburgh to the hunting. . . . . After this hunting he hanged John Armstrong, laird of Kilknocky, and his complices, to the number of thirty-six

gen - tle - man I sing a sang, Sum-tyme call'd laird of Gil - noc - kie. The king he wrytes a luv - ing let - ter, With his ain hand sae ten - der-

persons, for the which many Scotish men heavily lamented; for he was the most redoubted chiftain that had been for a long time on the Borders, either of Scotland or England. He rode ever with twenty-four able gentlemen, well horsed, yet he never molested any Scotish-man. But it is said that, from the Borders to Newcastle, every man, of whatsomever estate, paid him tribute to be free of his trouble. He came before the king, with his foresaid number richly apparelled, trusting that, in respect of his free offer of his person, he should obtain the king's favour. But the king, seeing him and his men so gorgeous in their apparel, with so many brave men under a tyrant's commandment, frowardly turning him about, he bade take the tyrant out of his sight, saying, 'What wants that knave that a king should have?' But John Armstrong made great offers to the king, That he should sustain himself, with forty gentlemen, ever ready at his service, on their own cost, without wronging any Scotish-man. *Secondly*, That there was not a subject in England, duke, earl, or baron, but within a certain day he should bring him to his majesty, either quick or dead. At length he, seeing no hope of favour, said, very proudly, 'It is folly to seek grace at a graceless face. But,' said he, 'had I known this, I should have lived on the Borders in despite of King Hary and you both; for I know King Hary would down-weigh my best horse with gold, to know that I were condemned to die this day."—Lindsay of Pitscottie's *History of Scotland*, p. 145. This execution is also noticed by Buchanan.

Armstrong's death appears to have been much talked of. In a sort of morality by Sir David Lindsay, entitled, "Ane Satyre of

ly, And he hath sent it to John-ie Arm-strang, To cum and speik with him speid-i-ly.

The Eliots and Armstrangs did convene;
They were a gallant company:
Weill ryde and meit our lawful king,
And bring him safe to Gilnockie.
Make kinnen and capon ready then,
And venison in great plenty,
Weill welcome hame our royal king,
I hope heill dyne at Gilnockie.

They ran their horse on the Langum " Howm,"
And brake their speirs with mckle main;

the Thrie Estaits," &c. Edin. 1602, 4to, a pardoner, enumerating the different relics in his possession, is made to say—

" Heir is ane coird baith great and lang,
    Quhilk hangit Johne the Armistrang,
        Of gude hemp soft and sound;
    Gude halie peopill I stand for'd,
    Quha evir beis hangit with this cord,
        Neids never to be dround."

This, which Ramsay calls " the true old ballad, never printed before," he copied, he tells us, " from a gentleman's mouth of the name of Armstrang," who was the sixth generation from the above John. The gentleman told him "this was ever esteemed the genuine ballad, the common one, false."

By " the common one," it is presumed, the gentleman meant the English song, which the reader may see in the " Select Collection," vol. ii., p. 112.

The ladys lukit frae their loft windows:
    God bring our men weil back again!
Quhen Johnie came before the king,
    With all his men sae brave to see,
The king he movit his bonnet to him,
    He weind he was a king as well as he.

May I find grace, my sovereign liege,
    Grace for my loyal men and me;
For my name it is Johnie Armstrang,
    And subject of zours, my liege, said he.
Away, away, thou traytor strang,
    Out of my sicht thou may'st sune be;
I grantit nevir a traytor's lyfe,
    And now I'll not begin with thee.

Grant me my lyfe, my liege, my king,
    And a bonnie gift I will give to thee,
Full four-and-twenty milk-whyt steids
    Were a' foald in a zeir to me.
I'll gie thee all these milk-whyt steids,
    That prance and nicher at a speir,
With as mekle gude Inglis gilt
    As four of their braid backs dow beir.
Away, away, thou traytor, &c.

Grant me my lyfe, my liege, my king,
    And a bonnie gift I'll gie to thee,
Gude four-and-twenty ganging mills,
    That gang throw a' the zeir to me.

These four-and-twenty mills complete,
    Sall gang for thee throw all the zeir,
And as mekle of gude reid quheit
    As all thair happers dow to bear.
Away, away, thou traytor, &c.

Grant me my lyfe, my liege, my king,
    And a great gift I'll gie to thee,
Bauld four and twenty sister's sons,
    Sall for thee fecht tho' all sould flee.
Away, away, thou traytor, &c.

Grant me my lyfe, my liege, my king,
    And a brave gift I'll gie to thee;
All betwene heir and Newcastle town
    Sall pay thair zeirly rent to thee.
Away, away, thou traytor, &c.

Ze leid, ze leid now, king, he says,
    Althocht a king and prince ze be;
For I luid naithing in all my lyfe,
    I dare well sayit, but honesty:
But a fat horse, and a fair woman,
    Twa bonnie dogs to kill a deir;
But Ingland suld haif found me meil and malt,
    Gif I had lived this hundred zeir.

Scho suld have found me meil and malt,
    And beif and mutton in all plentie;
But neir a Scots wyfe could haif said
    That eir I skaith'd her a pure flie.

To seik het water beneath cauld yce,
　　Surely it is a great folie;
I haif ask'd grace at a graceless face,
　　But there is nane for my men and me.

But had I kend, or I came frae hame,
　　How thou unkynd wadst bene to me,
I wad haif kept the Border syde,
　　In spyte of all thy force and thee.
Wist England's king that I was tane,
　　O gin a blyth man wald he be!
For anes I slew his sister's son,
　　And on his breist-bane brak a tree.

John wore a girdle about his midle,
　　Imbroider'd owre with burning gold,
Bespangled with the same mettle,
　　Maist beautifull was to behold.
Ther hang nine targats at Johnie's hat,
　　And ilk an worth three hundred pound:
What wants that knave that a king suld haif,
　　But the sword of honour and the crown?

O quhair gat thou these targats, Johnie,
　　That blink sae brawly abune thy brie?
I gat them in the field fechting,
　　Quher, cruel king, thou durst not be.
Had I my horse and my harness gude,
　　And ryding as I wont to be,
It sould haif bene tald this hundred zeir
　　The meiting of my king and me.

God be withee, Kirsty, my brither,
    Lang live thou Laird of Mangertoun,
Lang may'st thou dwell on the Border-syde,
    Or thou se thy brither ryde up and doun.
And God be withee, Kirsty, my son,
    Quhair thou sits on thy nurse's knee;
But and thou live this hundred zeir,
    Thy father's better thou 'lt never be.

Farweil, my bonny Gilnockhall,
    Quhair on Esk-syde thou standest stout,
Gif I had lived but seven zeirs mair,
    I wald haif gilt thee round about.
John murdred was at Carlinrigg,*
    And all his galant companie;
But Scotland's heart was never sae wae,
    To see so many brave men die.

---

* "Carlinrig is about ten miles above Hawick, near the head of the water of Teviot; where, according to our best historians, this chieftain and his brave men were hanged on growing trees. The particular spot upon which these trees grew is yet well known to some of our old people, who scruple not to tell us, that, as a token of the king's injustice in this affair, the trees from that day withered away. It is said that one of John's attendants, by the strength and swiftness of his horse, forced his way through the many thousands that surrounded them, and carried the news of the unhappy fate of his master and companions to Gilnockie Castle, which then stood upon a rock, encompassed by the water of Esk, at a place now known by the name of the Hollows, a few miles below the Longholm."—*Poetical Museum*, Hawick, 1784.

Buchanan, who represents Armstrong to have been equally formidable to the Scots and the English, says that he was enticed to have recourse to the king, and that coming unarmed, with about fifty horse, without a safe-conduct, he fell into an ambush, and

Because they saved their country deir
Frae Englishmen; nane were sae bauld,
Quhyle Johnie liv'd on the border syde,
Nane of them durst cum neir his hald.

SONG IV.

THE BATTLE OF CORICHIE, ON THE HILL OF FAIR,
FOUGHT OCT. 28, 1562.*

BY JOHN FORBES,
SCHOOLMASTER AT MARY CULTER, UPON DEESIDE.

Murn ye heighlands, and murn ye leigh-lands, I trow ye hae mei-kle need; For thi bon-ny burn of Co-ri-chie His run this day wi' bleid?

was brought to the king as a prisoner. Lord Hailes thinks that "Buchanan obliquely censures James V. for this great act of public justice." His Lordship is, however, mistaken in supposing JOHN THE REIF to mean JOHNY ARMSTRONG. See *Ancient Scottish Poems*, Edin., 1770, p. 265.

Armstrong's death is likewise related by Bishop Lesley, who adds an instance of horrid cruelty—the wife and children of one of the sufferers being burnt alive in his house. He also says that George Armstrong, brother to John, saved his life by turning informer. *De R. G. Scotorum*, Romæ, 1578, p. 403.

* For a further account of this battle, see Buchanan, Spotswood, Hume of Godscroft, and Gordon's History of the Gordons.

Thi hopefu' Laird o' Finliter,
    Erle Huntly's gallant son,
For thi love hi bare our beauteous quine,
    His gart fair Scotland mone.

Hi his braken his ward in Aberdene
    Throu dreid o' thi fause Murry;
And his gather't the gentle Gordone clan,
    An' his father auld Huntly.

Fain wad he tak our bonny guide quine,
    An' beare hir awa' wi' him;
But Murry's slee wyles spoil't a' thi sport,
    An' reft him o' lyfe and lim.

Murry gar't rayse thi tardy Merns men,
    An Angis, an' mony ane mair;
Erle Morton, and the Byres Lord Lindsay;
    An' campit at thi Hill o' Fare.

Erle Huntlie came wi' Haddo Gordone,
    An' countit ane thusan men;
But Murry had abien twal hunder,
    Wi' sax score horsemen and ten.

They soundit thi bougills an' the trumpits,
    An' marchit on in brave array;
Till the spiers an' the axis forgatherit,
    An' than did begin thi fray.

Thi Gordones sae fercelie did fecht it,
    Withouten terrer or dreid,
That mony o' Murry's men lay gaspin',
    An' dyit thi grund wi' theire bleid.

Then fause Murry feingit to flee them,
    An' they pursuit at his backe,
Whan thi haf o' thi Gordones desertit,
    An' turnit wi' Murray in a crack.

Wi' hether i' thir bonnits they turnit,
    The traiter Haddo o' their heid,
An' slaid theire brithers an' their fatheris,
    An' spoilit an' left them for deid.

Than Murry cried to tak thi auld Gordone,
    An' mony ane ran wi' speid;
But Stuart o' Inchbraik had him stickit,
    An' out gushit thi fat lurdane's bleid.

Than they tuke his twa sones quick an' hale,
    An' bare them awa' to Aberdene;
But sair did our guide quine lament
    Thi waefu' chance that they were tane.

Erle Murry lost mony a gallant stout man,
    Thi hopefu' Laird o' Thornitune,
Pittera's sons, an Egli's far fearit laird,
    An' mair to mi unkend, fell doune.

Erle Huntly mist tenscore o' his bra' men
    Sum o' heigh, an' sum o' leigh degree;
Skeenis youngest son, thi pride o' a' the clan,
    Was ther fun' dead, he widna flee.

This bloody fecht wis fercely faucht
    Octobris aught an' twinty day,
Crystis fyfteen hundred thriscore yeir
    An' twa will mark thi deidlie fray.

But now the day maist waefu' came,
    That day the quine did grite her fill,
For Huntly's gallant stalwart son,
    Wis heidit on the heidin' hill.

Fyve noble Gordones wi' him hangit were,
    Upon thi samen fatal playne;
Crule Murry gar't thi waefu' quine luke out,
    And see hir lover an' liges slayne.

I wis our quine had better frinds,
    I wis our countrie better peice;
I wis our lords wid na' discord,
    I wis our weirs at hame may ceise.

SONG V.

"ADAM" OF GORDON.*

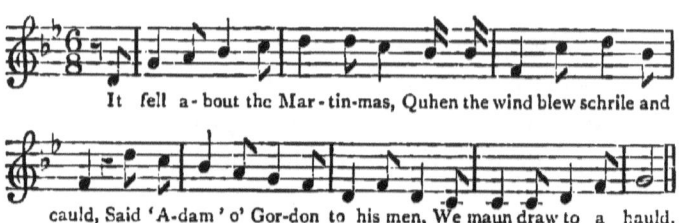

It fell a-bout the Mar-tin-mas, Quhen the wind blew schrile and cauld, Said 'A-dam' o' Gor-don to his men, We maun draw to a hauld.

And what an a hauld sall we draw to,
My merry men and me?
We will gae to the house of the Rodes,
To see that fair ladie.

---

* The story of this song is as follows: In the year 1571, Sir Adam Gordon of Auchindown, brother to the Earl of Huntly, whose deputy he was in the north parts, where, as Archbishop Spotswood relates, "under colour of the queen's authority, [he] committed divers oppressions, especially upon the Forbes's," "had sent one Captain Ker, with a party of foot, to summon the castle of Towie [or Tavoy, as Spotswood calls it] in the queen's name. The owner, Alexander Forbes, was not then at home, and his lady, confiding too much in her sex, not only refused to surrender, but gave Ker very injurious language; upon which, unreasonably transported with fury, he ordered his men to fire the castle, and barbarously burnt the unfortunate gentlewoman, with her whole family, amounting to 37 persons. Nor was he ever so much as cashiered for this inhuman action, which made Gordon share both in the scandal and the guilt."—Crawford's *Memoirs*, Edin., 1753, p. 213. So that it evidently appears that the writer of this ballad, either through ignorance or design, has made use of Gordon's name instead of Ker's; and there is some reason to think the transposition intentional. A ballad upon this subject, in the English idiom, and written about the time, which nearly resembles that here printed, so

She had nae sooner busket hersel',
  Nor putten on her gown,
Till "Adam" o' Gordon and his men
  Were round about the town.

They had nae sooner sitten down,
  Nor sooner said the grace,
Till "Adam" o' Gordon and his men
  Were closed about the place.

The lady ran up to her tower head,
  As fast as she could drie,
To see if by her fair speeches
  She could with him agree.

As soon as he saw the lady fair,
  And hir yates all locked fast,
He fell into a rage of wrath,
  And his heart was aghast.

nearly, indeed, as to make it evident that one of them must be an alteration from the other, is still extant; in which ballad, instead of Adam or Edom o' Gordon, we have "Captain Care," who is called "the lord of Easter towne," the castle of Rodes is "the castle of Crecrynbroghe," and the lady's husband is a "lord Hamleton." In other respects they are so much alike, that Bishop Percy, finding, as he says, an (apparently incorrect) fragment of the English ballad in his folio MS., "improved and enlarged" (*i.e.*, interpolated and corrupted) the Scotish copy "with several fine stanzas." See the English ballad at length, in a collection of *Ancient English Songs*, published by J. Johnson, in St Paul's Church Yard.

It has been usual to entitle this ballad "Edom o' Gordon;" an error which Sir David Dalrymple, to whom, as Bishop Percy says, we are indebted for its publication, might be led into by the local pronunciation of the lady from whose memory he gave it.

Cum down to me, ze lady fair,
    Cum down to me, let 's see,
This night ze's ly by my ain side,
    The morn my bride sall be.

I winnae cum down, ye fals Gordon,
    I winnae cum down to thee,
I winnae forsake my ane dear lord,
    That is sae far frae me.

Gi up your house, ze fair lady,
    Gi up your house to me,
Or I will burn zoursel' therein,
    Bot you and zour babies three.

I winnae gie up, zou fals Gordon,
    To nae sic traitor as thee,
Tho' zou should burn mysel' therein,
    Bot and my babies three.

Set fire to the house, quoth fals Gordon,
    Sin better may nae bee,
And I will burn hersel' therein,
    Bot and her babies three.

And ein wae worth ze, Jock, my man,
    I paid ze weil zour fee;
Why pow ze out my ground wa' stane,
    Lets in the reek to me?

And ein wae worth ze, Jock, my man,
    For I paid zou weil zour hire;
Why pow ze out my ground wa' stane,
    To me lets in the fire?

Ye paid me weil my hire, lady,
    Ye paid me weil my fee:
But now I'm "Adam" of Gordon's man,
    Maun either do or die.

O then bespake her zoungest son,
    Sat on the nurse's knee,
Dear mother, gie owre your house, he says,
    For the reek it worries me.

I winnae gie up my house, my dear,
    To nae sik traitor as he;
Cum well, cum wae, my jewels fair,
    Ye maun tak share wi' me.

O then bespake her dochter dear,
    She was baith jimp and sma',
O row me in a pair o' shiets,
    And tow me owre the wa'.

They row'd her in a pair of shiets,
    And tow'd her owre the wa',
But, on the point of "Adam's" speir,
    She gat a deadly fa'.

O bonny, bonny was hir mouth,
    And chirry were her cheiks,
And clear, clear was hir zellow hair,
    Whereon the reid bluid dreips.

Then wi' his speir he turn'd hir owre,
    O gin hir face was wan!
He said, zou are the first that e'er
    I wist alive again.

He turn'd her owre and owre again;
    O gin hir skin was whyte!
He said, I might ha' spared thy life,
    To been some man's delyte.

Busk and boon, my merry men all,
    For ill dooms I do guess,
I cannae luik in that bonny face,
    As it lyes on the grass.

Them luiks to freits, my master deir,
    Then freits will follow them;
Let it neir be said brave "Adam" o' Gordon
    Was daunted with a dame.

O then he spied hir ain deir lord,
    As he came owre the lee;
He saw his castle in a fire,
    As far as he could see.

Put on, put on, my mighty men,
    As fast as ze can drie,
For he that's hindmost of my men,
    Sall neir get guid o' me.

And some they raid, and some they ran
    Fu' fast out owre the plain,
But lang, lang e'er he coud get up,
    They were a' deid and slain.

But mony were the mudie men
    Lay gasping on the grien;
For o' fifty men that "Adam" brought out
    There were but five ged heme.

And mony were the mudie men
    Lay gasping on the grien;
And mony were the fair ladys
    Lay lemanless at heme.

And round, and round the wa's he went,
    Their ashes for to view;
At last into the flames he flew,
    And bad the world adieu.

SONG VI.

GILDEROY.*

BY SIR ALEXANDER HALKET.

Gil-de-roy was a bon-ny boy, Had ros-es tu'l his shoone, His stock-ings were of silk-en soy, Wi' gar-ters hang-ing doune; It was, I weene, a come-lie sight, To see sae trim a boy; He was my jo and heart's de-light, My hand-some Gil-de-roy.

* A hero of whom this elegant lamentation is the only authentic memorial. He hence appears to have been a celebrated Highland freebooter, and to have been executed at Edinburgh in the time of Queen Mary. The author's name is prefixed on the authority of Johnston's *Scot's Musical Museum.*

Oh! sik twa charming een he had,
  A breath as sweet as rose,
He never ware a Highland plaid,
  But costly silken clothes:
He gain'd the luve of ladies gay,
  Nane eir tul him was coy:
Ah! wae is me! I mourn the day,
  For my dear Gilderoy.

My Gilderoy and I were born
  Baith in one toun together,
We scant were seven years beforn
  We gan to luve each other;
Our dadies and our mammies thay
  Were fill'd wi' mickle joy
To think upon the bridal day
  'Twixt me and Gilderoy.

For Gilderoy that luve of mine,
  Gude faith I freely bought
A wedding sark of holland fine,
  Wi' silken flowers wrought;
And he gied me a wedding ring,
  Which I received wi' joy:
Nae lad nor lassie eir could sing
  Like me and Gilderoy.

Wi' mickle joy we spent our prime,
  Till we were baith sixteen,
And aft we past the langsome time
  Amang the leaves sae green;

Aft on the banks we 'd sit us thair,
    And sweetly kiss and toy,
Wi' garlands gay wad deck my hair,
    My handsome Gilderoy.

Oh that he still had been content
    Wi' me to lead his life!
But, ah! his manfu' heart was bent
    To stir in feates of strife;
And he in many a venturous deed
    His courage bauld wad try,
And now this gars mine heart to bleed
    For my dear Gilderoy.

And whan of me his leave he tuik,
    The tears they wat mine ee,
I gave tul him a parting luik,
    "My benison gang wi' thee!
God speid thee weil, mine ain dear heart,
    For gane is all my joy;
My heart is rent sith we maun part,
    My handsome Gilderoy."

My Gilderoy baith far and near
    Was fear'd in every town,
And bauldly bare away the gear
    Of many a Lawland loun:
Nane eir durst meet him man to man,
    He was sae brave a boy,
At length wi' numbers he was tane,
    My winsome Gilderoy.

The Queen of Scots possessed nought
   That my love let me want;
For cow and ew he to me brought,
   And een whan they were skant:
All these did honestly possess
   He never did annoy,
Who never fail'd to pay their cess
   To my love Gilderoy.

Wae worth the loun that made the laws
   To hang a man for gear!
To reave of life for ox or ass,
   For sheep, or horse, or mare!
Had not their laws been made sae strick,
   I neir had lost my joy,
Wi' sorrow neir had wat my cheek
   For my dear Gilderoy.

Gif Gilderoy had done amisse,
   He mought hae banisht been,
Ah! what sair cruelty is this,
   To hang sik handsome men!
To hang the flower o' Scotish land,
   Sae sweet and fair a boy!
Nae lady had sae white a hand
   As thee, my Gilderoy.

Of Gilderoy sae 'fraid they were,
   They bound him mickle strong,
Tul Edenburrow they led him thair,
   And on a gallows hung;

372 SCOTISH SONGS.

They hung him high aboon the rest,
   He was sae trim a boy,
Thair dyed the youth whom I lo'ed best,
   My handsome Gilderoy.

Thus having yielded up his breath,
   I bare his corpse away,
Wi' tears that trickled for his death
   I washt his comelye clay;
And siker in a grave sae deep,
   I laid the dear-lo'ed boy;
And now for evir maun I weep
   My winsome Gilderoy.

SONG VII.

THE BONNY EARL OF MURRAY.*

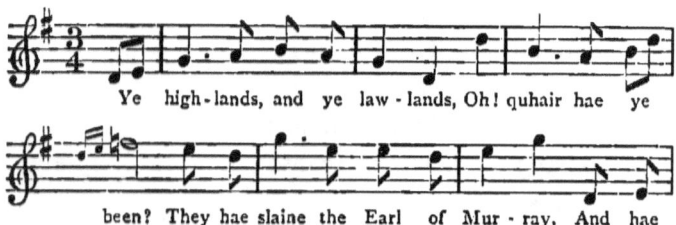

Ye high-lands, and ye law-lands, Oh! quhair hae ye been? They hae slaine the Earl of Mur-ray, And hae

---

* "In December 1591, Francis Stewart, Earl of Bothwell, had made an attempt to seize the person of his sovereign, James VI., but being disappointed, had retired towards the North. The king unadvisedly gave a commission to George Gordon, Earl of Huntley, to pursue Bothwell and his followers with fire and sword. Huntley, under cover of executing that commission, took occasion to revenge a private quarrel he had against James Stewart, Earl of Murray, a relation of Bothwell's. In the night of February 7, 1592, he beset

lain him on the green; They hae slaine the Earl of Mur-ray, And hae lain him on the green.

> Now wae be to thee, Huntley!
> And quhairfore did you sae?
> I bade you bring him wi' you,
> But forbade you him to slay.
>
> He was a braw gallant,
> And he rid at the ring;
> And the bonny Earl of Murray,
> Oh! he might hae been a king.

Murray's house, burnt it to the ground, and slew Murray himself; a young nobleman of the most promising virtues, and the very darling of the people.

"The present Lord Murray hath now in his possession a picture of his ancestor, naked and covered with wounds, which had been carried about, according to the custom of that age, in order to inflame the populace to revenge his death. If this picture did not flatter, he well deserved the name of the BONNY EARL, for he is there represented as a tall and comely personage. It is a tradition in the family that Gordon of Buckie gave him a wound in the face: Murray, half expiring, said, 'You hae spilt a better face than your awin.' Upon this Bucky, pointing his dagger at Huntley's breast, swore, 'You shall be as deep as I,' and forced him to pierce the poor defenceless body.

"King James, who took no care to punish the murtherers, is said by some to have privately countenanced and abetted them, being stimulated by jealousy for some indiscreet praises which his queen had too lavishly bestowed on this unfortunate youth."—PERCY.

He was a braw gallant,
  And he play'd at the ba';
And the bonny Earl of Murray
  Was the flower among them a'.

He was a braw gallant,
  And he play'd at the gluve;
And the bonny Earl of Murray,
  Oh! he was the queene's luve.

Oh! lang will his lady
  Luke owre the castle downe,
Ere she see the Earl of Murray
  Cum sounding throw the towne.

SONG VIII.

FRENNET HALL.*

When Fren-net cas-tle's i-vied walls, Thro' yal-low leaves were seen, When birds for-sook the sap-less boughs,

---

* The subject of this ballad is related by W. Gordon, in his *History of the Illustrious Family of Gordon*, 1726, vol. ii. p. 135, in the following words:—

"*Anno* 1630, there happened a melancholy accident to the family of Huntly thus: First of January there fell out a discord betwixt the laird of Frendraught and some of his friends, and William Gordon of Rothemay and some of his, in which William Gordon

And bees the fad-ed green, Then La-dy Fren-net, venge-ful dame, Did wan-der frae the ha', To the wild for-est's dew-ie gloom, 'A-mong the leaves that fa'.

was killed, a brave and gallant gentleman. On the other side was slain George Gordon, brother to Sir James Gordon of Lesmore, and divers others were wounded on both sides. The Marquis of Huntley and some other well-disposed friends made up this quarrel; and Frendraught was appointed to pay to the lady dowager of Rothemay 50,000 merks Scots, in compensation of the slaughter, which, as is said, was truly paid . . . .

"Upon the 27th of September this year, Frendraught having in his company Robert Chrichton of Coudlaw, and James Lesly, son to the laird of Pitcaple, Chrichton shot Lesly through the arm, who was carried to his father's house, and Frendraught put Chrichton out of his company. Immediately thereafter he went to visit the Earl of Murray; and, in his return, came to the Bog of Gight, now Castle-Gordon, to visit the Marquis of Huntly; of which Pitcaple getting notice, . . . conveens about 30 horsemen, fully armed, and with them marches to intercept Frendraught, and to be revenged of him for the hurt his son had got. He came to the marquis's house, October 7. Upon which the marquis wisely desired Frendraught to keep company with his lady, and he would discourse Pitcaple, who complained to him grievously of the harm he had done to his son, and vowed he would be revenged of him ere he returned home. The marquis did all he could to excuse Frendraught, and satisfy Pitcaple, but to no purpose; and so he went away in a chaff, still

Her page, the swiftest of her train,
Had clumb a lofty tree,
Whase branches to the angry blast
Were soughing mournfullie :

He turn'd his een towards the path
That near the castle lay,
Where good Lord John and Rothemay
Were riding down the brae.

vowing revenge. The marquis communicated all that had passed to Frendraught, and kept him at his house a day or two ; and even then would not let him go home alone, but sent his son, John Gordon, Viscount of Melgum and Aboyne, with some others, as a safeguard to him, until he should be at home, (among whom was John Gordon of Rothemay, son to him lately slain,) lest Pitcaple should lie in ambush for him.

"They convoyed him safely home, and after dinner Aboyne pressed earnestly to return ; and as earnestly did Frendraught press him to stay, and would by no means part with him that night. He at last condescended to stay, though unwillingly. They were well entertained, supped merrily, and went to bed joyful. The viscount was laid in a room in the old tower of the hall, standing upon a vault, where there was a round hole under his bed ; Robert Gordon and English Will, two of his servants, were laid beside him ; the laird of Rothemay, and some servants by him, in an upper room above Aboyne ; and above that, in another room, George Chalmers of Noth, and another of the viscount's servants ; all of them lodged in that old tower, and all of them in rooms one above the other. All of them being at rest, about midnight the tower takes fire, in so sudden and furious a manner, that this noble lord, the laird of Rothemay, English Will, Colin Ivat, and other two, being six in number, were cruelly burnt to death, without help or relief offered to be made ; the laird and lady looking on, without so much as endeavouring to deliver them from the fury of those merciless flames, as was reported.

"Robert Gordon, who was in Aboyne's chamber, escaped, as ('tis

Swift darts the eagle from the sky,
    When prey beneath is seen;
As quickly he forgot his hold,
    And perch'd upon the green.

O hie thee, hie thee, lady gay,
    Frae this dark wood awa;
Some visitors of gallant mein
    Are hasting to the ha'.

said) Aboyne might have done, if he had not rushed up-stairs to awake Rothemay; and while he was about that, the wooden passage and the lofting of the room took fire, so that none of them could get down-stairs. They went to the window that looked into the court, and cried many times help for God's sake, the laird and lady looking on; but all to no purpose. And finally, seeing there was no help to be made, they recommended themselves to God, clasped in one another's embraces. And thus perished in those merciless flames the noble Lord John Gordon, Viscount of Melgum and Aboyne, and John Gordon of Rothemay, a very brave youth. This viscount was a very complete gentleman, both in body and mind, and much lamented by the whole country, but especially by his father, mother, and lady, who lived a melancholy and retired life all her time thereafter. And this was all the reward the Marquis of Huntley got for his good-will to Frendraught, says my author Spalding, who lived not far from the place, and had the account from eye-witnesses."

This Sir James Crichton, laird of Frendraught, was, in 1642, created Viscount Frendraught. His lady was Elizabeth Gordon, daughter of John Earl of Sutherland, and near cousin to the Marquis of Huntley. In revenge for this treacherous and horrid act, the law not affording any redress, Frendraught's estates were repeatedly ravaged by the Gordons, and his cattle and sheep slaughtered or sold. Gordon adds: "The family of Frendraught was then a very opulent family; they had a great land-estate and much money; and after that it soon went to ruin, and was some time ago extinct."

The present ballad appears to have been suggested by one composed at the time, a few stanzas of which are fortunately remembered by the Rev. Mr Boyd, translator of *Dante*, and were obligingly

>   Then round she row'd her silken plaid,
>   Her feet she did na spare,
>   Untill she left the forest skirts
>   A lang bow-shot and mair.

communicated to the editor by his very ingenious and valuable friend, J. C. Walker, Esq.

>   The reek it rose, and the flame it flew,
>   And oh! the fire augmented high,
>   Until it came to Lord John's chamber-window,
>   And to the bed where Lord John lay.
>
>   O help me, help me, Lady Frennet,
>   I never ettled harm to thee,
>   And if my father slew thy lord,
>   Forget the deed and rescue me.
>
>   He looked east, he looked west,
>   To see if any help was nigh;
>   At length his little page he saw,
>   Who to his lord aloud did cry,
>
>   Loup down, loup down, my master dear,
>   What though the window's dreigh and hie,
>   I'll catch you in my arms twa,
>   And never a foot from you I'll flee.
>
>   How can I loup, you little page?
>   How can I leave this window hie?
>   Do you not see the blazing low,
>   And my twa legs burnt to my knee?

"There are some intermediate particulars," Mr Boyd says, "respecting the lady's lodging her victims in a turret or flanker, which did not communicate with the castle. This," adds he, "I only have from tradition, as I never heard any other stanzas besides the foregoing." The author of the original, we may perceive, either through ignorance or design, had deviated from the fact in supposing Lady Frennet's husband to have been slain by Lord John's father; and perhaps also in representing the two youths as brothers. The actual provocation appears to have been the payment of the 50,000 merks, the price of Rothemay's blood; which sort of compensation, Gordon has remarked, seems not to prosper, that family being then extinct.

O where, O where, my good Lord John,
 O tell me where you ride?
Within my castle-wall this night
 I hope you mean to bide.

Kind nobles, will ye but alight,
 In yonder bower to stay,
Saft ease shall teach you to forget
 The hardness of the way.

Forbear entreaty, gentle dame,
 How can we here remain?
Full well you ken your husband dear
 Was by our father slain.

The thoughts of which with fell revenge
 Your angry bosom swell;
Enraged you've sworn that blood for blood
 Should this black passion quell.

O fear not, fear not, good Lord John,
 That I will you betray,
Or sue requital for a debt
 Which nature cannot pay.

Bear witness, a' ye powers on high,
 Ye lights that 'gin to shine,
This night shall prove the sacred cord
 That knits your faith and mine.

SCOTISH SONGS.

The lady slee, with honey'd words,
Enticed thir youths to stay:
But morning sun nere shone upon
Lord John nor Rothemay.

SONG IX.

GENERAL LESLY'S MARCH TO LONGMASTON MOOR.*

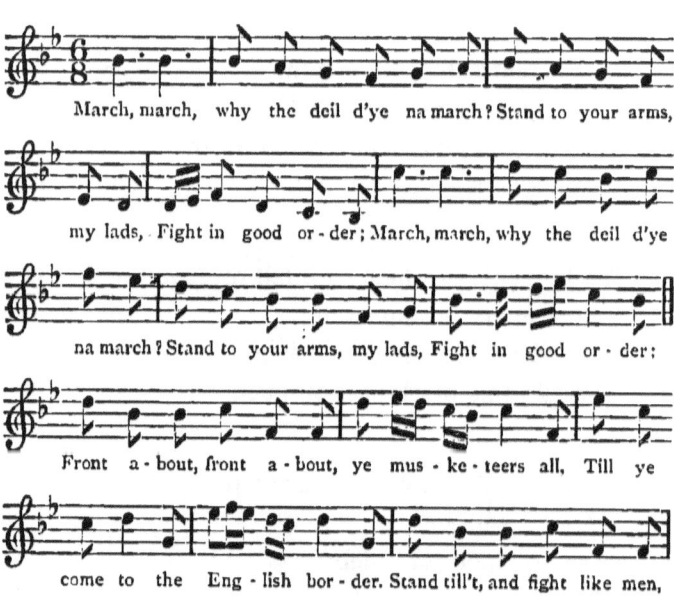

March, march, why the deil d'ye na march? Stand to your arms, my lads, Fight in good or-der; March, march, why the deil d'ye na march? Stand to your arms, my lads, Fight in good or-der: Front a-bout, front a-bout, ye mus-ke-teers all, Till ye come to the Eng-lish bor-der. Stand till't, and fight like men,

* Alexander Lesly (created, in 1641, Earl of Leven) invaded England, at the head of the Scotish rebel army, in 1640, defeated a party of the king's troops, and took possession of Newcastle. He afterward commanded the army sent by the Covenanters to the assistance of the Parliament, and contributed greatly to the defeat of the Royalists at Marston (here meant by Longmaston)-moor, in Yorkshire, 3d July 1644.

SONG X.

THE HAWS OF CROMDALE.*

As I came in by A-chen-down, A lit-tle we bit frae the town, When to the High-lands I was bown, To view the haws of Crom-dale, I met a man in tar-tan trews, I spier'd at him what was the news; Quoth he, The High-land ar-my rues That e'er we came to Crom-dale.

We were in bed, sir, every man,
When the English host upon us came;
A bloody battle then began,
    Upon the haws of Cromdale.

---

* No notice is taken of this battle in the history of Montrose's wars, nor does any mention of it elsewhere occur. The only action known to have happened at Cromdale (a village in Inverness-shire) was long after Montrose's time; although the circumstance of the English army falling upon the Highlanders in bed makes it highly probable that this is the action alluded to.

The English horse they were so rude,
They bathed their hoofs in Highland blood,
But our brave clans they boldly stood
        Upon the haws of Cromdale.

But, alas! we could no longer stay,
For o'er the hills we came away,
And sore we do lament the day
        That e'er we came to Cromdale.

Thus the great Montrose did say,
Can you direct the nearest way?
For I will o'er the hills this day,
        And view the haws of Cromdale.

Alas! my lord, you're not so strong,
You scarcely have two thousand men,
And there's twenty thousand on the plain,
        Stand rank and file on Cromdale.

Thus the great Montrose did say,
I say, direct the nearest way,
For I will o'er the hills this day,
        And see the haws of Cromdale.

They were at dinner, every man,
When great Montrose upon them came,
A second battle then began
        Upon the haws of Cromdale.

The Grants, Mackenzies, and Mackay,
Soon as Montrose they did espy,
O then they fought most vehemently
      Upon the haws of Cromdale.

The M'Donalds they return'd again,
The Camerons did their standard join,
M'Intosh play'd a bonny game
      Upon the haws of Cromdale.

The M'Gregors faught like lyons bold,
M'Phersons, none could them controul,
M'Lauchlins faught like loyal souls,
      Upon the haws of Cromdale.

[M'Leans, M'Dougals, and M'Neals,
So boldly as they took the field,
And made their enemies to yield,
      Upon the haws of Cromdale.]

The Gordons boldly did advance,
The Fraziers [fought] with sword and lance,
The Grahams they made their heads to dance,
      Upon the haws of Cromdale.

The loyal Stewarts, with Montrose,
So boldly set upon their foes,
And brought them down with Highland blows,
      Upon the haws of Cromdale.

Of twenty thousand Cromwell's men,
Five hundred went to Aberdeen,
The rest of them lyes on the plain,
　　Upon the haws of Cromdale.

SONG XI.

GILLICRANKIE.*

Cla-vers and his High-land-men Came down up-o' the raw, man, Who, be-ing stout, gave mo-ny a clout, The lads be-gan to claw then. Wi' sword and terge in-to their hand, Wi' which they were nae slaw, man, Wi' mo-ny a fear-ful hea-vy sigh, The lads be-gan to claw then.

* The battle of Killiecrankie was fought, at the pass so called, on the 27th of July 1689, between the Highland clans, under the command of James (Graham of Claverhouse) Viscount Dundee, and a Dutch-English army commanded by General Mackay. The latter were almost instantaneously defeated, with a very inconsiderable loss

O'er bush, o'er bank, o'er ditch, o'er stank,
    She flang amang them a', man;
The Butter-box got mony knocks,
    Their riggings paid for a' then.
They got their paiks, wi' sudden straikes,
    Which to their grief they saw, man;
Wi' clinkum clankum o'er their crowns,
    The lads began to fa' then.

Hur skipt about, hur leapt about,
    And flang amang them a', man;
The English blades got broken heads,
    Their crowns were cleaved in twa then.
The durk and door made their last hour,
    And proved their final fa', man;
They thought the devil had been there,
    That play'd them sic a paw then.

The solemn league and covenant
    Came whigging up the hills, man,
Thought Highland trews durst not refuse
    For to subscribe their bills then:
In Willie's* name they thought nae ane
    Durst stop their course at a', man;
But hur nane-sell, wi' mony a knock,
    Cry'd, Furich-whiggs, awa', man.

on the other side, if we except that of their gallant leader, who received a mortal wound under his arm, elevated in the act of encouraging his men to the pursuit. King James felt his loss irretrievable.

    * Prince of Orange.

Sir Evan Du, and his men true,
    Came linking up the brink, man,
The Hogan Dutch they feared such,
    They bred a horrid stink then.
The true Maclean, and his fierce men,
    Came in amang them a', man ;
Nane durst withstand his heavy hand,
    All fled and ran awa' then.

Oh' on a ri, oh' on a ri,
    Why should she lose King Shames, man?
Oh' rig in di, oh' rig in di,
    She shall break a' her banes then ;
With *furichinish,* an' stay a while,
    And speak a word or twa, man,
She 's gi' a straike, out o'er the neck,
    Before ye win awa' then.

O fy for shame ! ye 're three for ane,
    Hur nane-sell 's won the day, man ;
King Shames' red-coats should be hung up,
    Because they ran awa' then :
Had bent their brows, like Highland trows,
    And made as lang a stay, man,
They'd saved their king, that sacred thing,
    And Willie 'd run awa' then.

SONG XII.*

Carl, an the king come, Carl, an the king come; Thou shalt dance and I will sing, Carl, an the king come. An some-bo-die were come a-gain, Then some-bo-die maun cross the main, And ev'-ry man shall hae his ain, Carl, an the king come.

    I trow we swapp'd for the worse,
    We gae the boot and better horse ;
    And that we'll tell them at the cross,
      Carl, an the king come.

* The exact age of this song has not been ascertained ; and perhaps it is here inserted under too early a period. There are probably other words to this air, as the following stanza has been recovered by accident :—

      When yellow corn grows on the rigs,
      And a gibbet's made to hang the Whigs,
      O then we will dance Scotish jigs,
        Carle, au the king come.

Coggie, an the king come,
Coggie, an the king come,
I'se be fou, and thou'se be toom,
Coggie, an the king come.

SONG XIII.

ON THE ACT OF SUCCESSION, (1703.*)

TUNE—"Woo'd and married and a'." †

I'LL sing you a song, my brave boys,
  The like you ne'er heard of before,
Old Scotland at last is grown wise,
  And England shall bully no more.

Succession, the trap for our slavery,
  A true Presbyterian plot,
Advanced by by-ends and knavery,
  Is now kick'd out by a vote.

The Lutheran dame ‡ may be gone,
  Our foes shall addresse us no more,

* "The Earl of Marchmont having one day presented an act for settling the succession in the house of Hanover, it was treated with such contempt, that some proposed it might be burnt, and others that he might be sent to the castle, and was at last thrown out of the house by a plurality of fifty-seven voices."—Lockhart's *Memoirs*, p. 60.   † Page 275.
‡ Sophia Electress-Dowager of Hanover, mother of George I.

If the treaty* should never go on,
   She for ever is kick'd out of door.

To bondage we now bid adieu,
   The English shall no more oppresse us,
There's something in every man's view
   That in due time we hope shall redresse us.

These hundred years past we have been
   Dull slaves, and ne'er strove to mend;
It came by an old barren queen,
   And now we resolve it shall end.

But grant the old woman should come,
   And England with treaties should wooe us,
We'll clog her before she comes home,
   That she ne'er shall have power to undoe us.

Then let us goe on and be great,
   From parties and quarrells abstain;
Let us English councills defeat,
   And Hanover ne'er mention again.

Let grievances now be redress'd,
   Consider the power is our own;
Let Scotland no more be oppress'd,
   Nor England lay claim to our crown.

    * For the union of the two kingdoms.

Let us think with what blood and what care
    Our ancestors kept themselves free;
What Bruce and what Wallace could dare;
    If they did so much, why not we?

Let Montrose and Dundee be brought in
    As latter examples before you;
And hold out but as you begin,
    Like them the next age will adore you.

Here's a health, my brave lads, to the duke[*] then,
    Who has the great labour begun,
He shall flourish, whilst those who forsook him
    To Holland for shelter shall run.

Here's a health to those that stood by him,
    To Fletcher,[†] and all honest men;
Ne'er trust the damn'd rogues that belie 'em,
    Since all our rights they maintain.

Once more to great Hamilton's health,
    The hero that still keeps his ground;
To him we must own all our wealth:—
    Let the Christian liquor go round.

---

[*] James Duke of Hamilton; able, spirited, and unsteady. He was killed 15th November 1812, in a duel with Lord Mohun, and, as was thought, by General Macartney, that nobleman's second; he himself falling at the same time.

[†] Andrew Fletcher of Saltoun, Esquire; a warm and strenuous advocate for republican government, and the natural rights of mankind. He has left a volume of excellent political discourses.

Let all the sham tricks of the court,
That so often have foil'd us before,
Be now made the countrie's sport,
And England shall fool us no more.

SONG XIV.

THE THISTLE AND ROSE.

BY MR WATT.

It was in old times, when trees com-posed rhymes, And flowers did with e-le-gy flow, It was in a field, which vari-ous did yield, A Rose and a This-tle did grow. In a sun-shin-ing day, the Rose chanced to say, Friend This-tle, I'll be with you plain, And if you would be but u-nit-ed with me, You would ne'er be a This-tle a-gain.

Says the Thistle, my spears shield mortals from fears,
    Whilst thou dost unguarded remain;
And I do suppose, though I were a Rose,
    I would long to be a Thistle again.
O friend, says the Rose, you falsely suppose,
    Bear witness, ye flowers of the plain!
You would take so much pleasure, in beauty's vast treasure,
    You would ne'er be a Thistle again.

The Thistle at length, admiring the Rose,
    With all the gay flowers of the plain,
She throws off her points, herself she anoints,
    And now in close Union she's gone.
But in a cold stormy day, while heedless she lay,
    No longer could sorrow refrain,
She fetched a groan, with many ohon,
    O were I a Thistle again!

For then I did stand on yon heath-cover'd land,
    Admired by each nymph and each swain;
And free as the air I flourish'd there,
    The terror and pride of the plain.
But now I'm the mock of Flora's fair flock,
    Nor dare I presume to complain;
But remember that I disasterly cry,
    O were I a Thistle again!

SONG XIV.*

SUCH A PARCEL OF ROGUES IN A NATION.

BY ROBERT BURNS.

Fare-weel to a' our Scot-ish fame, Fare-weel our an-cient glo-ry; Fare-weel e-ven to the Scot-ish name, Sae famed in mar-tial sto-ry! Now Sark rins o'er the Sol-way sands, And Tweed rins to the o-cean, To mark where Eng-land's pro-vince stands; Such a par-cel of rogues in a na-tion!

What force or guile could not subdue,
Through many warlike ages,
Is wrought now by a coward few,
For hireling traitors' wages.

The English steel we could disdain,
  Secure in valour's station,
But English gold has been our bane:
  Such a parcel of rogues in a nation!

O would, or I had seen the day
  That treason thus could sell us,
My auld gray head had lien in clay,
  Wi' Bruce and loyal Wallace!
But pith and power, till my last hour
  I 'll mak this declaration,
We 're bought and sold for English gold:
  Such a parcel of rogues in a nation!

SONG XV.

LITTLE WAT YE WHA'S COMING.*

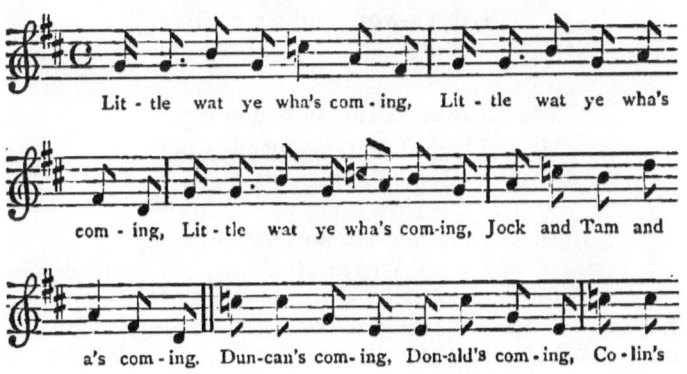

Lit-tle wat ye wha's com-ing, Lit-tle wat ye wha's com-ing, Lit-tle wat ye wha's com-ing, Jock and Tam and a's com-ing. Dun-can's com-ing, Don-ald's com-ing, Co-lin's

* The Chevalier's Muster Roll, 1715.

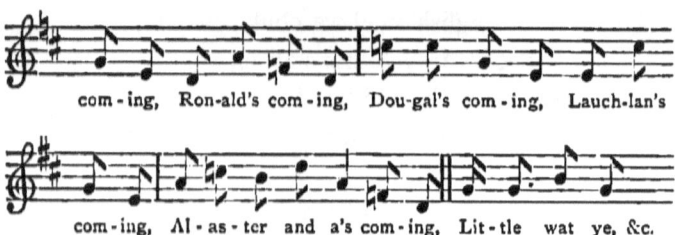

Borland and his men 's coming,
The Camrons and M'Leans' coming,
The Gordons and M'Gregors' coming,
A' the Dunywastles' * coming :
    Little wat ye wha 's coming,
    M'Gilvrey of Drumglass is coming.

Wigton's coming, Nithsdale's coming,
Carnwarth's coming, Kenmure's coming,
Derwentwater and Foster's coming,
Withrington and Nairn's coming : †
    Little wat ye wha 's coming,
    Blyth Cowhill and a's coming.

The laird of M'Intosh is coming,
M'Crabie and M'Donald's coming,

---

* *i.e.*, Highland lairds or gentlemen; *Dhuine wasal*.

† These are the Earls of Wigton, Nithisdale, and Carnwath, the Viscount Kenmure, the Earl of Derwentwater, Thomas Foster, Esquire, member of parliament for Northumberland, and commander-in-chief of the Chevalier's English army, the Earl of Widdrington, and the Lord Nairn : the other names are either those of particular clans, or such as are applicable to all.

The M'Kenzies and M'Phersons' coming,
A' the wild M'Craws' coming:
  Little wat ye wha's coming,
  Donald Gun and a's coming.

They gloom, they glowr, they look sae big,
At ilka stroke they'll fell a Whig;
They'll fright the fuds of the pockpuds,
For many a buttock bare's coming:
  Little wat ye wha's coming,
  Jock and Tam and a's coming.

———◆———

SONG XV.*

O KENMURE'S ON AND AWA, WILLIE.†

COMPOSED IN PART BY ROBERT BURNS.

O Ken-mure's on and a-wa, Wil-lie, O Ken-mure's on and a-wa: An Ken-mure's lord's the brav-est lord That ev-er Gal-lo-way

† William Gordon, Viscount Kenmure, was commander-in-chief of the Chevalier's forces in the south of Scotland. Having joined General Forster, and marched to Preston in Lancashire, he there surrendered himself a prisoner at discretion, and was (very unjustly, as some thought) beheaded on Tower-hill, 24th February 1716.

saw. Suc-cess to Ken-mure's band, Wil-lie! Suc-cess to Ken-mure's band! There's no a heart that fears a Whig That rides by Ken-mure's hand.

 Here's Kenmure health in wine, Willie,
  Here's Kenmure's health in wine;
 There ne'er was a coward o' Kenmure's blude,
  Nor yet o' Gordon's line.

 O Kenmure's lads are men, Willie,
  O Kenmure's lads are men;
 Their hearts and swords are metal true,
  And that their faes shall ken.

 They'll live or die wi' fame, Willie,
  They'll live or die wi' fame;
 But soon wi' sounding victorie
  May Kenmure's lord come hame!

 Here's him that's far awa, Willie,
  Here's him that's far awa;
 And here's the flower that I lo'e best,
  The rose that's like the snaw.

SONG XVI.

SHERIFF-MUIR.*

BY THE REV. MURDOCH M'LENNAN OF CRATHIE.

There's some say that we wan, Some say that they wan, Some say that nane wan at a', man; But one thing I'm sure, That at Sher-iff-Muir A bat-tle there was, which I saw, man; And we ran, and they ran, and they ran, and we ran, and we ran, and they ran a-wa', man.

* The battle of Dumblain or Sheriff-Muir was fought the 13th of November 1715, between the Earl of Mar, for the Chevalier, and the Duke of Argyle, for the Government. Both sides claimed the victory, the left wing of either army being routed. The capture of Preston, it is very remarkable, happened on the same day.

Brave Argyle* and Belhaven,†
Not like frighted Leven,‡
Which Rothes§ and Haddington|| sa', man ;
For they all with Wightman¶.
Advanced on the right, man,
While others took flight, being ra', man.

Lord Roxburgh** was there,
In order to share
With Douglas††, who stood not in awe, man,
Volunteerly to ramble
With Lord Loudoun Campbell,‡‡
Brave Ilay§§ did suffer for a', man.

Sir John Schaw,|||| that great knight,
With broad-sword most bright,

---

* John (Campbell) second Duke of Argyle, commander-in-chief of the Government forces; a nobleman of great talents and integrity, much respected by all parties: died 1743.

† John (Hamilton) Lord Belhaven: served as a volunteer, and had the command of a troop of horse raised by the county of Haddington: perished at sea, 1721.

‡ David (Lesly) Earl of Leven; for the Government.

§ John (Lesly) Earl of Rothes; for the Government.

|| Thomas (Hamilton) Earl of Haddington; for the Government.

¶ Major-General Joseph Wightman.

** John (Ker) first Duke of Roxburghe; for the Government.

†† Archibald (Douglas) Duke of Douglas.

‡‡ Hugh (Campbell) Earl of Loudon.

§§ Archibald Earl of Ilay, brother to the Duke of Argyle. He was dangerously wounded.

|||| An officer in the troop of gentlemen volunteers.

On horseback he briskly did charge, man;
    An hero that's bold,
    None could him with-hold,
He stoutly encounter'd the targemen.

    For the cowardly Whittam,*
    For fear they should cut him,
Seeing glittering broad-swords with a pa', man,
    And that in such thrang,
    Made Baird edicang,†
And from the brave clans ran awa', man.

    The great Colonel Dow
    Ga'ed foremost, I trow,
When Whittam's dragoons ran awa', man,
    Except Sandy Baird,
    And Naughton the laird,
Their horse show'd their heels to them a', man.

    Brave Mar ‡ and Panmure §
    Were firm, I am sure,
The latter was kidnapt awa', man,
    With brisk men about,
    Brave Harry ‖ retook
His brother, and laught at them a', man.

* Major-General Thomas Whitham.
† *i.e.*, Aide-de-camp.
‡ John (Erskine) Earl of Mar, commander-in-chief of the Chevalier's army; a nobleman of great spirit, honour, and abilities. He died at Aix-la-Chapelle in 1732.
§ James (Maule) Earl of Panmure; died at Paris 1723.
‖ Honourable Henry Maule, brother to the Earl. The circumstance here alluded to is thus related in the Earl of Mar's printed

2 C

Grave Marshall* and Lithgow,†
And Glengarys ‡ pith too,
Assisted by brave Logie A'mon, §
And Gordons the bright
So boldly did fight,
The red-coats took flight, and awa', man.

Strathmore ‖ and Clanronald ¶
Cry'd still, Advance, Donald!
Till both these heroes did fa', man ;**

account of the engagement:—"The prisoners taken by us were very civilly used, and none of them stripped. Some were allowed to return to Stirling upon their parole, &c. . . . . The few prisoners taken by the enemy on our left were most of them stripped and wounded after taken, the Earl of Panmure being first of the prisoners wounded after taken. They having refused his parole, he was left in a village, and by the hasty retreat of the enemy, upon the approach of our army, was rescued by his brother and his servants."

* George (Keith) Earl Marischall, then a youth at college. He died at his government of Neufchatel in 1778. His brother, the celebrated Marshall Keith, was with him in this battle.

† James (Livingston) Earl of Calendar and Linlithgow: attainted.

‡ Alexander M'Donald of Glengary, laird of a clan; a brave and spirited chief: attainted.

§ Thomas Drummond of Logie-Almond; commanded the two battalions of Drummonds. He was wounded.

‖ John (Lyon) Earl of Strathmore; "a man of good parts, of a most amiable disposition and character."

¶ Ranald M'Donald, captain of Clan-Ranald. *N.B.*—The captain of a clan was one who, being next or near in blood to the chief, headed them in his infancy or absence.

** "We have left, to our regret, the Earl of Strathmore and the Captain of Clan-Ranald."—Earl of Mar's Letter to the Governor of Perth. Again, printed account :—"We cannot find above sixty of our men in all killed, among whom were the Earl of Strathmore

For there was such hashing,
And broad-swords a clashing,
Brave Forfar* himself got a cla', man.

Lord Perth † stood the storm,
Seaforth ‡ but lukewarm,
Kilsyth § and Strathallan ‖ not sla', man;
And Hamilton ¶ pled
The men were not bred,
For he had no fancy to fa', man.

[and] the Captain of Clan-Ranald, both much lamented." The latter, "for his good part and gentle accomplishments, was looked upon as the most gallant and generous young gentleman among the clans. . . . . He was lamented by both parties that knew him."

His servant, who lay on the field watching his dead body, being asked next day who that was, answered, He was a man yesterday. —Boswell's *Journey to the Hebrides*, p. 359.

* Archibald (Douglas) Earl of Forfar, who commanded a regiment in the duke's army. He is said to have been shot in the knee, and to have had ten or twelve cuts in his head from the broadswords. He died a few days after of his wounds.

† James Marquis of Drummond, son of James (Drummond) Duke of Perth, was lieutenant-general of horse, and "behaved with great gallantry." He was attainted, but escaped to France, where he soon after died.

‡ William (Mackenzie) Earl of Seaforth. He was attainted, and died in 1740.

§ William (Livingston) Viscount Kilsyth: attainted.

‖ William (Drummond) Viscount Strathallan; whose sense of loyalty could scarcely equal the spirit and activity he manifested in the cause. He was taken prisoner in this battle, which he survived to perish in the still more fatal one of Culloden-Muir.

¶ Lieutenant-General George Hamilton, commanding under the Earl of Mar.

Brave generous Southesk,*
Tilebairn† was brisk,
Whose father indeed would not dra', man,
Into the same yoke,
Which served as a cloak,
To keep the estate 'twixt them twa, man

Lord Rollo,‡ not fear'd,
Kintore § and his beard,
Pitsligo ‖ and Ogilvie ¶ a', man,
And brothers Balfours,**
They stood the first showers,
Clackmannan and Burleigh †† did cla', man.

* James (Carnegie) Earl of Southesk; was attainted, and, escaping to France, died there in 1729.

† William (Murray) Marquis of Tullibardine, eldest son to the Duke of Athol. Having been attainted, he was taken at sea in 1746, and died soon after, of a flux, in the Tower.

‡ Robert (Rollo) Lord Rollo; "a man of singular merit and great integrity:" died in 1758.

§ William (Keith) Earl of Kintore.

‖ Alexander (Forbes) Lord Pitsligo; a man of good parts, great honour and spirit, and universally beloved and esteemed." He was engaged again in the affair of 1745, for which he was attainted, and died at an advanced age in 1762.

¶ James Lord Ogilvie, eldest son of David (Ogilvie) Earl of Airly. He was attainted, but afterwards pardoned. His father, *not dra'ing into the same yoke*, saved the estate.

** Some relations, it is supposed, of the Lord Burleigh.

†† Robert (Balfour) Lord Burleigh. He was attainted, and died in 1757.

But Cleppan * acted pretty,
And Strowan the witty, †
A poet that pleases us a', man;
For mine is but rhime,
In respect of what's fine,
Or what he is able to dra', man.

For Huntly ‡ and Sinclair, §
They both plaid the tinclair,
With consciences black like a cra', man.
Some Angus and Fifemen
They ran for their life, man,
And ne'er a Lot's wife there at a', man.

Then Laurie the traytor,
Who betray'd his master,
His king and his countrie and a', man,
Pretending Mar might
Give order to fight,
To the right of the army awa', man. ‖

* Major William Clephane, adjutant-general to the Marquis of Drummond.

† Alexander Robertson of Struan; who, having experienced every vicissitude of life, with a stoical firmness, died in peace 1749. He was an excellent poet, and has left elegies worthy of Tibullus.

‡ Alexander (Gordon) Marquis of Huntly, eldest son to the Duke of Gordon, who, according to the usual policy of his country, (of which we here meet with several other instances,) remained neutral. —See Hume's History.

§ John Sinclair, Esq., commonly called Master of Sinclair, eldest son of Henry Lord Sinclair; was attainted, but afterwards pardoned, and died in 1750. The estate was preserved, of course.

‖ "There was at this time a report prevailed that one Drummond went to Perth under the notion of a deserter from the Duke of

Then Laurie, for fear
Of what he might hear,
Took Drummond's best horse and awa', man,
Instead of going to Perth,
He cross'd the Firth,
Alongst Stirling Bridge and awa', man.

To London he press'd,
And there he address'd,
That he behaved best of them a', man;
And there without strife
Got settled for life,
An hundred a year to his fa', man.

In Borrowstounness
He resides with disgrace,

Argyle, but in reality acted the part of a spy, and gave his Grace intelligence of all the motions of the enemy. This man was employed the day of the action as aide-de-camp to the Lord Drummond, and in that quality attended the Earl of Mar to receive his orders; the earl, when he found his right was like to break the duke's left, sent this Drummond with orders to General Hammilton, who commanded on the rebels' left, to attack the enemy briskly, for that he was like to get the better on the right. But Drummond, as they pretend, gave contrary orders, and intelligence to General Hammilton, acquainting him that the earl's right was broke, and desiring the general to retire with all the expedition possible, and in the best order he could. Upon which General Hammilton gave orders to slacken the attack, which was obeyed. Then, the duke's right approaching, the most of them gave way without striking a stroke, and those who stood were mostly gentlemen and officers, who were severely galled by the duke; and they pretend that Drummond, after performing this treacherous part, went over to the duke."—Campbell's *Life of John Duke of Argyle*, p. 204.

Till his neck stand in need of a dra', man,
And then in a tether
He'll swing from a ladder,
[And] go off the stage with a pa', man.

Rob Roy* stood watch
On a hill for to catch
The booty for ought that I sa', man,
For he ne'er advanced
From the place he was stanced,
Till no more to do there at a', man.

* " Among other causes of the rebels' misfortune in that day they reckon the part that Rob Roy M'Gregor acted to be one ; this Rob Roy, or [Red] Robert, was brother to the laird of M'Gregor, and commanded that clan in his brother's absence, but in the day of battle he kept his men together at some distance without allowing them to engage, though they showed all the willingness imaginable, and waited only an opportunity to plunder, which was, it seems, the chief of his design of coming there. This clan are a hardy rough people, but noted for pilfering, as they lie upon the border of the Highlands, and this Rob Roy had exercised their talents that way pretty much in a kind of thieving war he carried on against the Duke of Montrose, who had, as he alleged, cheated him of a small feudal estate."—Campbell's *Life of John Duke of Argyle*, p. 205.

The conduct of this gentleman (who, the historian would not tell us, had assumed the surname of Campbell, his own being prohibited by Act of Parliament) was the more surprising, as he had ever been remarked for courage and activity. When desired by one of his own officers to go and assist his friends, he is reported to have said, " If they cannot do it without me, they cannot do it with me." It is more than probable, however, that his interference would have decided the fortune of that day in favour of his own party. " He continued in arms for some years after, and committed great depredations in the shires of Dumbarton and Lennox, particularly on the Duke of Montrose's lands, defeating several detachments sent to reduce him."—Boyse's *History of the Rebellion*. He is in the number of those attainted by parliament.

So we all took the flight,
And Moubray the wright;
But Letham the smith was a bra' man,
For he took the gout,
Which truly was wit,
By judging it time to withdra', man,

And trumpet M'Lean,
Whose brecks were not clean,
Through misfortune he happen'd to fa', man,
By saving his neck
His trumpet did break,
Came off without musick at a', man.*

So there such a race was,
As ne'er in that place was,
And as little chase was at a', man;
From other they run,
Without touk of drum;
They did not make use of a pa', man.

Whether we ran or they ran,
Or we wan or they wan,
Or if there was winnin' at a', man,
There's no man can tell,
Save our brave general,
Wha first began rinnin' awa', man.

---

* The particulars of this anecdote nowhere appear. The hero is supposed to be the same John M'Lean, trumpet, who was sent from Lord Mar, then at Perth, with a letter to the Duke of Argyle, at Stirling camp, on the 30th of October.—*Vide* "Original Letters," 1730. Two copies, however, printed not long after 1715, read, "And trumpet *Marine.*"

Wi' the Earl o' Seaforth,
And the Cock o' the North,*
But Florence ran fastest awa', man,
Save the laird o' Phineven,†
Wha swore to be even
Wi' ony general or peer o' them a', man.
    And we ran, and they ran, and they ran, and
    we ran, and we ran, and they ran awa', man.

SONG XVII.

A Dialogue between Will Lick-Ladle and Tom Clean-Cogue, twa shepherds wha were feeding their flocks on the Ochil Hills on the day the Battle of Sheriff-Muir was fought.

BY THE REV. JOHN BARCLAY.

The Chorus to be sung after every verse, to the tune of the "Camerons' March."

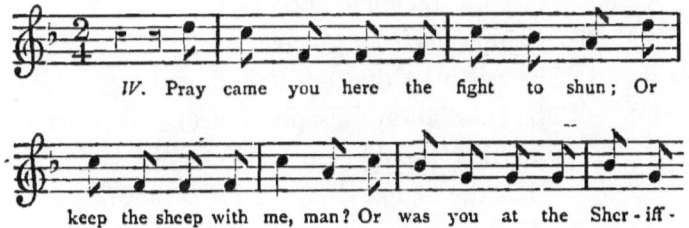

W. Pray came you here the fight to shun; Or keep the sheep with me, man? Or was you at the Sher-iff-

---

* An honorary popular title of the Duke of Gordon.
† Carnegy of Finhaven.

7. But, my dear Will, I kenna still,
    Whilk o' the twa did lose, man;
For well I wat they had good skill
    To set upo' their foes, man:
        The red-coats they are train'd, you see,
        The clans always disdain to flee,
        Wha then should gain the victory?
            But the highland race, all in a brace,
            With a swift pace, to the whigs' disgrace,
            Did put to chace
                    Their foes, man.

W. Now how deil, Tam, can this be true?
    I saw the chace gae North, man.
T. But well I wat they did pursue
    Them even unto Forth, man:
        Frae Dumblain they ran in my own sight,
        And got o'er the bridge with all their might,
        And those at Stirling took their flight;
            Gif only ye had been wi' me,
            You had seen them flee, of each degree,
            For fear to die
                      Wi' sloth, man.

W. My sister Kate came o'er the hill,
    Wi' crowdie unto me, man,
She swore she saw them running still
    Frae Perth unto Dundee, man.
        The left wing gen'ral had na skill,
        The Angus lads had no good will
        That day their neighbours' blood to spill;
            For fear by foes that they should lose
            Their cogues of brose, all crying woes,
            Yonder them goes,
                      D'ye see, man?

T. I see but few like gentlemen
    Amang yon frighted crew, man;
I fear my Lord Panmure be slain,
    Or that he's ta'en just now, man:
        For though his officers obey,
        His cowardly commons run away,
        For fear the red-coats them should slay;

　　　　The sodgers' hail make their hearts fail,
　　　　See how they scale, and turn their tail,
　　　　And rin to flail
　　　　　　　　And plow, man.

IV. But now brave Angus comes again
　　　Into the second fight, man;
　　They swear they'll either die or gain,
　　　No foes shall them affright, man:
　　　　Argyle's best forces they'll withstand,
　　　　And boldly fight them sword in hand,
　　　　Give them a general to command,
　　　　　A man of might, that will but fight,
　　　　　And take delight to lead them right,
　　　　　And ne'er desire
　　　　　　　　The flight, man.

　　But Flandrekins they have no skill
　　　To lead a Scottish force, man;
　　Their motions do our courage spill,
　　　And put us to a loss, man.
　　　　You'll hear of us far better news,
　　　　When we attack like Highland trews,
　　　　To hash, and slash, and smash and bruise,
　　　　　Till the field though braid be all o'erspread,
　　　　　But coat or plaid, wi' corpse that's dead,
　　　　　In their cold bed,
　　　　　　　　That's moss, man.

T. Twa gen'rals frae the field did run,
　　　Lords Huntley and Seaforth, man;

They cry'd and run grim death to shun,
   Those heroes of the North, man;*
     They 're fitter far for book or pen,
     Than under Mars to lead on men,
     Ere they came there they might well ken
        That female hands could ne'er gain lands,
        'Tis Highland brands that countermands
        Argathlean bands
                Frae Forth, man.

IV. The Camerons scower'd as they were mad,
   Lifting their neighbours' cows, man.
M'Kenzie and the Stewart fled,
   Without phil'beg or trews, man:
     Had they behaved like Donald's core,
     And kill'd all those came them before,
     Their king had gone to France no more:
        Then each Whig saint wad soon repent,
        And strait recant his covenant,
        And rent
                It at the news, man.

T. M'Gregors they far off did stand,
   Badenach and Athol too, man;
   I hear they wanted the command,
   For I believe them true, man.

---

* "They [*i. e.*, the insurgents] reckoned likewise that some noblemen and chiefs from the North did not act so honest a part, or at least did not shew so much courage as the zeal they expressed for the cause required."—Campbell's *Life of John Duke of Argyle*, p. 205.

Perth, Fife, and Angus, wi' their horse,
Stood motionless, and some did worse,
For, though the red-coats went them cross,
  They did conspire for to admire
  Clans run and fire, left wings retire,
  While rights entire
                Pursue, man.

IV. But Scotland has not much to say,
  For such a fight as this is,
Where baith did fight, baith ran away,
  The devil take the miss is
    That ev'ry officer was not slain
    That run that day, and was not ta'en,
    Either flying from or to Dumblain:
      When Whig and Tory, in their fury,
      Strove for glory, to our sorrow
      The sad story
                Hush is.

SONG XVIII.

UP AND WAR THEM A', WILLIE.

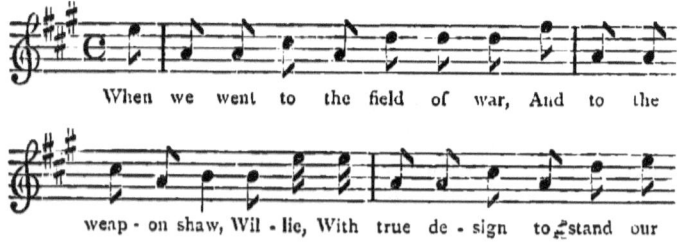

When we went to the field of war, And to the weap-on shaw, Wil-lie, With true de-sign to stand our

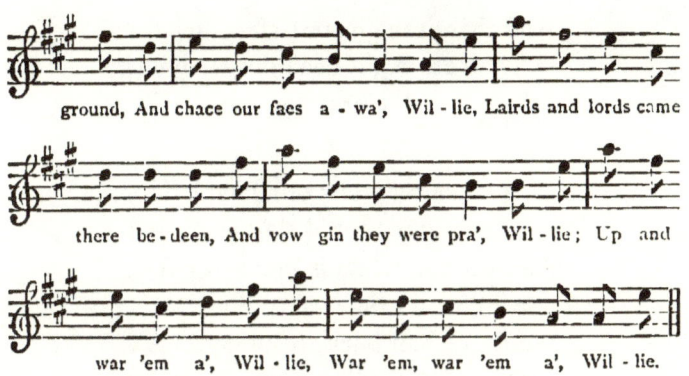

ground, And chace our faes a-wa', Wil-lie, Lairds and lords came there be-deen, And vow gin they were pra', Wil-lie; Up and war 'em a', Wil-lie, War 'em, war 'em a', Wil-lie.

And when our army was drawn up,
   The bravest e'er I saw, Willie,
We did not doubt to rax the rout,
   And win the day and a', Willie:
Pipers play'd frae right to left,
   Fy, fourugh Whigs awa', Willie.
      Up and war, &c.

But when our standard was set up,
   So fierce the wind did bla', Willie,
The golden knop down from the top,
   Unto the ground did fa', Willie:
Then second-sighted Sandy said,
   We'll do nae good at a', Willie.
      Up and war, &c.

When bra'ly they attack'd our left,
   Our front, and flank, and a', Willie,
Our bald commander on the green,
   Our faes their left did ca', Willie,

And there the greatest slaughter made
    That e'er poor Tonald saw, Willie.
        Up and war, &c.

First when they saw our Highland mob,
    They swore they'd slay us a', Willie;
And yet ane fyl'd his breiks for fear,
    And so did rin awa', Willie:
We drave him back to Bonnybrigs,
    Dragoons, and foot, and a', Willie.
        Up and war, &c.

But when their gen'ral view'd our lines,
    And them in order saw, Willie,
He straight did march into the town,
    And back his left did draw, Willie:
Thus we taught them the better gate,
    To get a better fa', Willie.
        Up and war, &c.

And then we rallied on the hills,
    And bravely up did draw, Willie:
But gin ye spear wha wan the day,
    I'll tell you what I saw, Willie:
We baith did fight, and baith were beat,
    And baith did rin awa', Willie.
So there's my canty Highland sang,
    About the thing I saw, Willie.*

---

* The copies of this and the preceding song, inserted in Johnson's *Scots Musical Museum*, contain great variations.

SONG XIX.

TRANENT-MUIR.*

BY ADAM SKIRVING.

TUNE — "Gillicrankie."

The Chevalier, being void of fear,
   Did march up Birstle brae, man,
And through Tranent, e'er he did stent,
   As fast as he could gae, man:
While General Cope did taunt and mock,
   Wi' mony a loud huzza, man;
But e'er next morn proclaim'd the cock,
   We heard another craw, man.

The brave Lochiel,† as I heard tell,
   Led Camerons on in clouds, man;
The morning fair, and clear the air,
   They loosed with devilish thuds, man:

---

* A field of battle, better known by the name of Prestonpans, where Prince Charles Stewart, commonly called the Young Chevalier, at the head of his Highland army, completely routed the English forces, under the command of Sir John Cope, who was afterward tried by a court-martial for his conduct in this battle, and acquitted. He is said to have left the field in such haste that he never once stopped his horse, nor looked back, till he got to Berwick-upon-Tweed, which is sixty or seventy miles off. This action happened September 22, 1745.

† Donald Cameron of Lochiel, chief of the clan Cameron, a gentleman of great bravery, and of the most amiable disposition. He was wounded at the battle of Culloden, and died in France colonel of a regiment, which his grateful master had procured him, as a small reward and compensation for his great services and misfortunes, —— 1748.

Down guns they threw, and swords they drew,
    And soon did chace them aff, man;
On Seaton-Crafts they buft their chafts,
    And gart them rin like daft, man.

The bluff dragoons swore blood and 'oons,
    They'd make the rebels run, man;
And yet they flee when them they see,
    And winna fire a gun, man:
They turn'd their back, the foot they brake,
    Such terror seized them a', man;
Some wet their cheeks, some fyl'd their breeks,
    And some for fear did fa', man.

The volunteers prick'd up their ears,
    And vow gin they were crouse, man:
But when the bairns saw't turn to earn'st,
    They were not worth a louse, man;
Maist feck gade hame; O fy for shame!
    They'd better stay'd awa', man,
Than wi' cockade to make parade,
    And do nae good at a', man.

Menteith* the great, when hersell shit,
    Un'wares did ding him o'er man;
Yet wad nae stand to bear a hand,
    But aff fu' fast did scour, man;

---

* The minister of Longformacus, a volunteer; who, happening to come, the night before the battle, upon a Highlander easing nature at Preston, threw him over, and carried his gun as a trophy to Cope's camp.

O'er Soutra hill, e'er he stood still,
  Before he tasted meat, man :
Troth he may brag of his swift nag,
  That bare him aff sae fleet, man.

And Simpson * keen, to clear the een
  Of rebels far in wrang, man,
Did never strive wi' pistols five,
  But gallop'd with the thrang, man :
He turn'd his back, and in a crack
  Was cleanly out of sight, man ;
And thought it best ; it was nae jest
  Wi' Highlanders to fight, man.

'Mangst a' the gang nane bade the bang
  But twa, and ane was tane, man ;
For Campbell rade, but Myrie † stay'd,
  And sair he paid the kain, man ;
Fell skelps he got, was war than shot
  Frae the sharp-edged claymore, man ;
Frae mony a spout came running out
  His reeking-het red gore, man.

* Another volunteer Presbyterian minister, who said he would convince the rebels of their error by the dint of his pistols ; having, for that purpose, two in his pockets, two in his holsters, and one in his belt.

† Mr Myrie was a student of physic from Jamaica ; he entered as a volunteer in Cope's army, and was miserably mangled by the broad-swords.

But Gard'ner* brave did still behave,
    Like to a hero bright, man;
His courage true, like him were few
    That still despised flight, man;
For king and laws, and country's cause,
    In honour's bed he lay, man;
His life, but not his courage, fled,
    While he had breath to draw, man.

And Major Bowle, that worthy soul,
    Was brought down to the ground, man;
His horse being shot, it was his lot
    For to get mony a wound, man:
Lieutenant Smith, of Irish birth,
    Frae whom he call'd for aid, man,
Being full of dread, lap o'er his head,
    And wadna be gainsaid, man.

He made sic haste, sae spur'd his beast,
    'Twas little there he saw, man;

---

* James Gardiner, colonel of a regiment of horse. This gentleman's conduct, however celebrated, does not seem to have proceeded so much from the generous ardour of a noble and heroic mind, as from a spirit of religious enthusiasm, and a bigoted reliance on the Presbyterian doctrine of predestination, which rendered it a matter of perfect indifference whether he left the field or remained in it. Being deserted by his troop, he was killed by a Highlander, with a Lochaber axe.

Colonel Gardiner having, when a gay young man, at Paris, made an assignation with a lady, was, as he pretended, not only deterred from keeping his appointment, but thoroughly reclaimed from all such thoughts in future, by an apparition. See his Life by Doddridge.

To Berwick rade, and safely said,
  The Scots were rebels a', man :
But let that end, for well 'tis kend
  His use and wont to lie, man ;
The Teague is naught, he never faught,
  When he had room to flee, man.

And Caddell drest, amang the rest,
  With gun and good claymore, man,
On gelding gray he rode that way,
  With pistols set before, man ;
The cause was good, he 'd spend his
    blood,
  Before that he would yield, man ;
But the night before he left the cor',
  And never faced the field, man.

But gallant Roger, like a soger,
  Stood and bravely fought, man ;
I 'm wae to tell, at last he fell,
  But mae down wi' him brought, man :
At point of death, wi' his last breath,
  (Some standing round in ring, man,)
On 's back lying flat, he waved his hat,
  And cry'd, God save the king, man.

Some Highland rogues, like hungry dogs,
  Neglecting to pursue, man,
About they faced, and in great haste
  Upon the booty flew, man ;

And they, as gain, for all their pain,
    Are deck'd wi' spoils of war, man;
Fu' bald can tell how her nainsell
    Was ne'er sae pra before, man.

At the thorn-tree, which you may see
    Be-west the meadow-mill, man,
There mony slain lay on the plain,
    The clans pursuing still, man.
Sic unco' hacks, and deadly whacks,
    I never saw the like, man;
Lost hands and heads cost them their
    deads,
    That fell near Preston-dyke, man.

That afternoon, when a' was done,
    I gaed to see the fray, man;
But had I wist what after past,
    I'd better stay'd away, man:
On Seaton sands, wi' nimble hands,
    They pick'd my pockets, bare, man;
But I wish ne'er to drie sick fear,
    For a' the sum and mair, man.

SONG XIX.*

THERE'LL NEVER BE PEACE TILL JAMIE COMES HAME.

BY ROBERT BURNS.

My seven braw sons for Jamie drew sword,
And now I greet round their green beds in the yerd;
It brak the sweet heart of my faithfu' auld dame:
There'll never be peace till Jamie comes hame.
Now life is a burden that bows me down,
Sin I tint my bairns, and he tint his crown;
But till my last moments my words are the same,
There'll never be peace till Jamie comes hame.

SONG XX.

COPE, ARE YOU WAKING YET?

TUNE—" Fy to the Hills in the Morning."

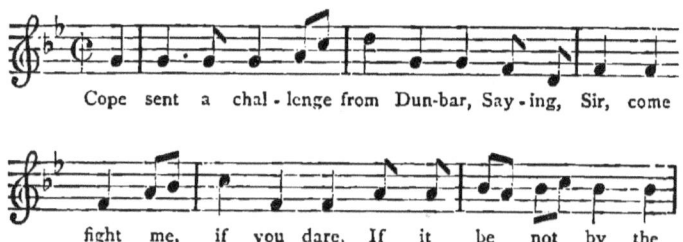

My merry men, come follow me,
For now's the time I'll let you see,
What a happy nation this will be,
And we'll visit Cope in the morning.

'Tis Cope, are you waking yet?
Or are you sleeping? I would wit;
'Tis a wonder to me when your drums beat,
It does not waken you in the morning.

The Highland men came down the loan,
With sword and target in their hand,
They took the dawning by the end,
And they visited Cope in the morning.

For all their bombs, and bomb-granades,
'Twas when they saw the Highland lads,
They ran to the hills as if they were calves,
And scour'd off early in the morning.

For all your bombs, and your bomb-shells,
'Tis when they saw the Highland lads,
They ran to the hills like frighted wolves,
All pursued by the clans in the morning.

The Highland knaves, with loud huzzas,
Cries, Cope, are you quite awa'?
Bide a little, and shake a pa',
And we'll give you a merry morning.

Cope went along unto Haddington,
They ask'd him where was all his men;
The pox on me if I do ken,
For I left them all this morning.*

---

* VARIATION.
JONNIE COUP.
BY ADAM SKIRVING.

Coup sent a challenge frae Dunbar,
Charlie, meet me an ye dare,
And I'll learn you the art of war,
If you'll meet wi' me in the morning.
 Hey Jonnie Coup, are ye waking yet?
 Or are your drums a beating yet?
 If ye were waking I would wait
 To gang to the coals i' the morning.

When Charlie look'd the letter upon,
He drew his sword the scabbard from,
Come follow me, my merry merry men,
And we'll meet Jonnie Coup i' the morning.
 Hey Jonnie Coup are ye waking yet, &c.

SONG XXI.

THE CLANS.

Tune—"The Campbells are coming."

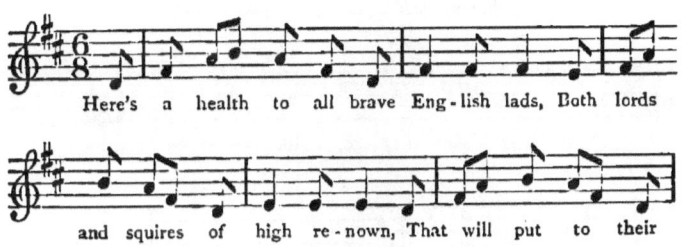

Here's a health to all brave Eng-lish lads, Both lords and squires of high re-nown, That will put to their

Now, Jonnie, be as good as your word,
Come let us try both fire and sword,
And dinna rin awa' like a frighted bird,
That's chased frae its nest in the morning.
    Hey Jonnie Coup, &c.

When Jonnie Coup he heard of this,
He thought it wadna be amiss
To hae a horse in readiness,
To flie awa' i' the morning.
    Hey Jonnie Coup, &c.

Fy now Jonnie get up and rin,
The Highland bagpipes makes a din,
It's best to sleep in a hale skin,
For 'twill be a bluddie morning.
    Hey Jonnie Coup, &c.

When Jonnie Coup to Dunbar came,
They spear'd at him, where's a' your men?
The deil confound me gin I ken,
For I left them a' i' the morning.
    Hey Jonnie Coup, &c.

Now, Jonnie, trouth ye was na blate,
To come wi' the news o' your ain defeat,
And leave your men in sic a strait,
So early in the morning.
    Hey Jonnie Coup, &c.

To set our king upon the throne,
    Not church nor state to overthrow,
As wicked preachers falsely tell,
    The clans are coming, oho, oho.
Therefore forbear ye canting crew,
    Your bugbear tales are but for show;
The want of stipends is your fear,
    And not the clans, oho, oho.

    Ah! faith, co' Jonnie, I got a fleg,
    With their claymores and philabegs,
    If I face them again, deil break my legs,
    So I wish you a good morning.
        Hey Jonnie Coup, &c.

In Johnson's *Scots Musical Museum*, Edin. 1787, &c., is a copy differing very much from both. One would wish to know the original, which, perhaps, is now impossible.

We will protect both church and state,
   Though they be held our mortal foe;
And when Hanover's to the gait,
   You'll bless the clans, oho, oho.
Corruption, brib'ry, breach of law,
   This was your cant some time ago,
Which did expose both court and king,
   And raised our clans, oho, oho.

Roused like a lion from his den,
   When he thought on his country's woe,
Our brave protector Charles did come,
   With all his clans, oho, oho.
These lions for their country's cause,
   And nat'ral prince were never slow;
So now they come with their brave prince,
   The clans advance, oho, oho.

And now the clans have drawn their swords,
   They vow revenge against them a',
That do lift up th' usurper's arms,
   To fight against our king and law.
Then God preserve our royal king,
   And his dear sons, the lovely twa,
And set him on his father's throne,
   And bless his subjects great and sma'.

SONG XXII.

THE WHITE COCKADE.

My love was born in A-ber-deen, The bon-niest land that e'er was seen, But now he makes our heart fu' sad, He takes the field wi' his white cock-ade. O he's a rant-ing, rov-ing lad, He is a brisk an' a bon-ny lad, Be-tide what may, I will be wed, And fol-low the boy wi' the white cock-ade.

  I'll sell my rock, my reel, my tow,
  My gude gray mare, and hawkit cow,
  To buy mysel a tartan plaid,
  To follow the boy wi' the white cockade.
    O he's a ranting, roving lad, &c.

SONG XXIII.

IN HONOUR OF THE MAYOR OF CARLISLE.*

Tune.—" Katherine Ogie."

Ye warlike men, with tongue and pen,
   Who boast such loud bravadoes,
And swear you 'll tame, with sword and flame,
   The Highland desperadoes,
Attend my verse, whilst I rehearse,
   Your modern deeds of glory,
And tell how Cope, the nation's hope,
   Did beat the rebel Tory.

With sword and targe, in dreadful rage,
   The mountain squires descended;
They cut and hack,—alack! alack!—
   The battle soon was ended:
And happy he who first could flee;
   Both soldiers and commanders
Swore in a fright, they'd rather fight
   In Germany or Flanders.

Some lost their wits, some fell in fits,
   Some stuck in bogs and ditches;
Sir John, aghast, like lightning past,
   Discharging in his breeches.

---

* Thomas Pattison, Esq. This city surrendered to the Chevalier, the 15th of November 1745, and was retaken by the Duke of Cumberland on the 31st of December following.—See the tune, page 127.

The blue-cap lads, with belted plaids,
    Syne scamper'd o'er the border,
And bold Carlisle, in humble style,
    Obey'd their leader's order.

O Pattison! ohon! ohon!
    Thou figure of a mayor!
Thou bless'd thy lot, thou wert no Scot,
    And bluster'd like a player:
What hast thou done, with sword or gun,
    To baffle the Pretender?
Of mouldy cheese and bacon-grease
    Thou much more fit defender.

Of front of brass, and brain of ass,
    With heart of hare compounded;
How are thy boasts repaid with costs,
    And all thy pride confounded!
Thou need'st not rave lest Scotland crave
    Thy kindred or thy favour,
Thy wretched race can give no grace,
    Nor glory thy behaviour.

SONG XXIV.

Tune—"The clans are coming." *

Let mournful Britons now deplore
  The horrors of Drummossie-day;
Our hopes of freedom all are o'er,
  The clans are all away, away.
The clemency so late enjoy'd,
  Converted to tyrannic sway,
Our laws and friends at once destroy'd,
  And forced the clans away, away.

His fate thus doom'd, the Scotish race
  To tyrants' lasting power a prey,
Shall all those troubles never cease?
  Why went the clans away, away?
Brave sons of Mars, no longer mourn,
  Your prince abroad will make no stay;
You'll bless the hour of his return,
  And soon revenge Drummossie-day.

* See before, page 427.

SONG XXV.

BY ALEXANDER ROBERTSON OF STRUAN, ESQ.

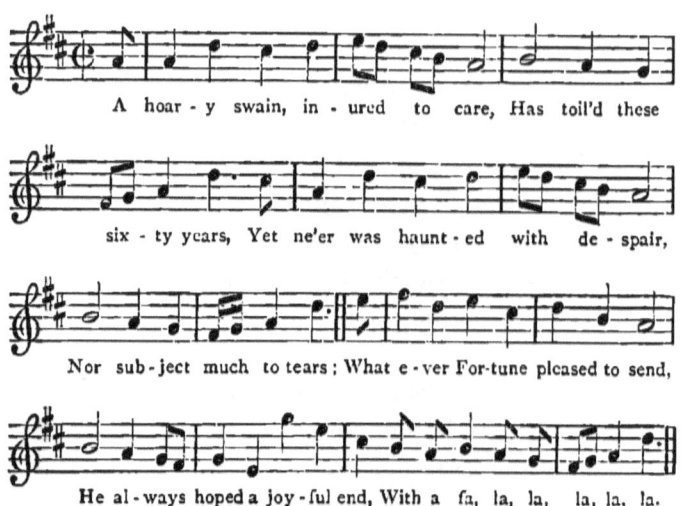

A hoar-y swain, in-ured to care, Has toil'd these six-ty years, Yet ne'er was haunt-ed with de-spair, Nor sub-ject much to tears; What e-ver For-tune pleased to send, He al-ways hoped a joy-ful end, With a fa, la, la, la, la, la.

He sees a champion of renown,
    Loud in the blast of fame,
For safety scouring up and down,
    Uncertain of his aim;
For all his speed, a ball from gun
Could faster fly than he could run.
        With a fa, la, &c.

Another, labouring to be great,
    By some is counted brave,
His will admits of no debate,
    Pronounced with look so grave;

Yet 'tis believed he is found out
Not quite so trusty as he's stout.
   With a fa, la, &c.

An action well contrived of late,
 Illustrates this my tale,
Where these two heroes tried their fate,
 In Fortune's fickle scale;
Where 'tis surmised they wisely sought,
In concert with each other's thought.
   With a fa, la, &c.

But first they knew that mountaineers,
 (As apt to fight as eat,)
Who once could climb the hills like deers,
 Now fainted without meat;
While English hearts, their hunger stanch,
Grew valiant as they cramm'd their paunch.
   With a fa, la, &c.

Thus fortified with beef and sleep,
 They waddling sought their foes,
Who scarce their eyes awake could keep,
 Far less distribute blows;
To whom we owe the fruits of this,
Inspect who will, 'tis not amiss.
   With a fa, la, &c.

Though we be sorely now opprest,
 By numbers driven from home,
Yet Fortune's wheel may turn at last,
 And Justice back may come;

In Providence we'll put our trust,
Which ne'er abandons quite the just.
   With a fa, la, &c.

E'en let them plunder, kill and burn,
 And on our vitals prey,
We'll hope for Charlie's safe return,
 As justly so we may;
The laws of God and man declare
The son should be the father's heir.
   With a fa, la, &c.

Let wretches, fluster'd with revenge,
 Dream they can conquer hearts,
The steady mind will never change,
 'Spite of their cruel arts:
We still have woods, and rocks, and men,
What they pull down to raise again.
   With a fa, la, &c.

And now let's fill the healing cup,
 Enjoin'd in sacred song,
To keep the sinking spirits up,
 And make the feeble strong;
How can the sprightly flame decline,
That always is upheld by wine?
   With a fa, la, la, la, la, la.

SONG XXVI.

AWA, WHIGS, AWA!

Our ancient crown's fa'n in the dust,
    Deil blin' them wi' the stoure o't;
And write his name in his black beuk
    Wha gae the Whigs the power o't.
        Awa, Whigs, &c.

Our sad decay in church and state
    Surpasses my descriving;
The Whigs cam o'er us for a curse,
    And we hae done wi' thriving.
        Awa, Whigs, &c.

Grim Vengeance lang has ta'en a nap,
    But we may see him wauken:
Gude help the day, when royal heads
    Are hunted like a maukin!
        Awa, Whigs, &c.

SONG XXVII.

WELCOME, CHARLEY STUART.

You're wel-come, Char-ley Stu-art, You're wel-come, Char-ley Stu-art, You're wel-come, Char-ley Stu-art, There's none so

right as thou art. Had I the pow-er to my will, I'd make thee fam-ous by my quill, Thy foes I'd scat-ter, take, and kill, From Bill-ings-gate to Du-art. You're wel-come, &c.

Thy sympathising complaisance
Made thee believe intriguing France;
But woe is me for thy mischance,
   Which saddens every heart.
        You're welcome, &c.

Hadst thou Culloden battle won,
Poor Scotland had not been undone,
Nor butcher'd been, with sword and gun,
   By Lockhart and such cowards.
        You're welcome, &c.

Kind Providence, to thee a friend,
A lovely maid did timely send,
To save thee from a fearful end,
   Thou charming Charley Stuart.
        You're welcome, &c.

Great glorious prince, we firmly pray
That she and we may see the day,

When Britons all with joy shall say,
You're welcome Charley Stuart.
    You're welcome, &c.

Though Cumberland, the tyrant proud,
Doth thirst and hunger after blood,
Just Heaven will preserve the good,
  To fight for Charley Stuart.
    You're welcome, &c.

Whene'er I take a glass of wine,
I drink confusion to the Swine,*
But health to him that will combine
  To fight for Charley Stuart.
    You're welcome, &c.

The ministry may Scotland maul,
But our brave hearts they'll ne'er enthrall;
We'll fight like Britons, one and all,
  For liberty and Stuart.
    You're welcome, &c.

Then haste, ye Britons, and set on
Your lawful king upon the throne;
To Hanover we'll drive each one
  Who will not fight for Stuart.
    You're welcome, &c.

    * The Duke of Cumberland.

SONG XXVIII.

Tune—"For a' that."

Though Geordie reigns in Jamie's stead, I'm grieved yet scorn to shaw that; I'll ne'er look down nor hang my head On rebel Whig for a' that; For still I trust that Providence Will us relieve from a' that; Our royal prince is weel in health, And will be here for a' that. For a' that, and a' that, And thrice as muckle as a' that; He's far beyond the seas the night, Yet he'll be here for a' that.

He's far beyond Dumblain the night,
Whom I love weel for a' that;
He wears a pistol by his side,
That makes me blyth for a' that;

The Highland coat, the philabeg,
    The tartan hose, and a' that;
And though he's o'er the seas the night,
    He'll soon be here for a' that.
        For a' that, &c.

He wears a broadsword by his side,
    And weel he kens to draw that,
The target and the Highland plaid,
    The shoulder-belt, and a' that;
A bonnet bound with ribbons blue,
    The white cockade, and a' that;
And though beyond the seas the night,
    Yet he'll be here for a' that.
        For a' that, &c.

The Whigs think a' that weal is won,
    But faith they maunna fa' that;
They think our loyal hearts dung down,
    But we'll be blyth for a' that.
For still we trust that Providence
    Will us relieve from a' that,
And send us hame our gallant prince,
    Then we'll be blyth for a' that.
        For a' that, &c.

But oh, what will the Whigs say syne,
    When they're mista'en in a' that,
When Geordie maun fling by the crown,
    His hat and wig, and a' that?

The flames will get baith hat and wig,
　As often they've done a' that;*
Our Highland lad will get the crown,
　And we'll be blyth for a' that.
　　　　For a' that, &c.

Oh! then your braw militia lads
　Will be rewarded duly,
When they fling by their black cockades,
　A hellish colour truly:
As night is banish'd by the day,
　The white shall drive awa' that;
The sun shall then his beams display,
　And we'll be blyth for a' that.
　　　　For a' that, &c.

* Alluding, perhaps, to a whimsical practice of King George II., which was to kick his hat and wig about the room, whenever he was in a passion.

" Concinet majore poeta plectro
――――, quandoque calens furore
Gestiet circa thalamum ferire
　　Calce galerum."
　　　　　　　　―LOVELING.

SONG XXIX.

Tune—"Alloa house." *

Oh! how shall I venture, or dare to reveal,
Too great for expression, too good to conceal,
The graces and virtues that illustriously shine
In the prince that's descended from the Stuart's great
    line!

Oh! could I extol, as I love the dear name,
And suit my low strains to my prince's high fame,
In verses immortal his glory should live,
And to ages unborn his merit survive.

But oh! thou great hero, just heir to the crown,
The world, in amazement, admires thy renown;
Thy princely behaviour sets forth thy just praise,
In trophies more lasting than poets can raise.

Thy valour in war, thy conduct in peace,
Shall be sung and admired, when division shall
    cease;
Thy foes in confusion shall yield to thy sway,
And those who now rule be compell'd to obey.

* See page 174.

SONG XXX.

CHARMING HIGHLANDMAN.*

BY DR ALEXANDER GEDDES.

Oh! send my Lew-is Gor-don hame, And the lad I dare na name; Al-though his back be at the wa',

Chorus.

Here's to him that's far a-wa'. Hech hey! my High-land-man! My hand-some, charm-ing High-land-man! Weel could I my true love ken, A-mang ten thou-sand High-land-men.

* This song is sometimes entitled "Lewis Gordon," and directed to be sung "To the tune of 'Tarry woo,'" of which the present is possibly but an alteration. (See p. 340.) Lord Lewis Gordon, younger brother to the then Duke of Gordon, commanded a detachment for the Chevalier, and acquitted himself with great gallantry and judgment. He died in 1754.

Oh, to see his tartan trouze,
Bonnet blue, and laigh-heel'd shoes,
Philabeg aboon his knee!
That's the lad that I 'll gang wi'.
   Hech hey! &c.

This lovely lad, of whom I sing,
Is fitted for to be a king;
And on his breast he wears a star,
You 'd take him for the god of war.
   Hech hey! &c.

Oh, to see this princely one
Seated on his father's throne!
Our griefs would then a' disappear,
We 'd celebrate the Jub'lee year.
   Hech hey! &c.

SONG XXXI.

STRATHALLAN'S LAMENT.*

BY ROBERT BURNS.

Thick - est night, sur - round my dwell - ing! Howl - ing

* Supposed to mean James Viscount Strathallan, whose father, Viscount William, was killed, as before mentioned, at the battle of Culloden. He escaped to France, and died in 1766.

In the cause of right engaged,
    Wrongs injurious to redress,
Honour's war we strongly waged,
    But the heavens denied success:
Ruin's wheel has driven o'er us,
    Not a hope that dare attend,
The wide world is all before us—
    But a world without a friend.

SONG XXXII.

MY HARRY* WAS A GALLANT GAY.

BY ROBERT BURNS.

Tune—"Highlander's Lament."

My Harry was a gallant gay, Fu' stately strade he on the plain, But now he's banish'd far away, I'll never see him back again. O for him back again! O for him back again! I wad gie a' Knockhaspie's land For Highland Harry back again.

When a' the lave gae to their bed,
I wander dowie up the glen;
I set me down and greet my fill,
And aye I wish him back again.
   O for him, &c.

* Henry Stuart, brother of the Chevalier.

O were some villains hangit high,
And ilka body had their ain!
Then I might see the joyful sight,
My Highland Harry back again.
O for him, &c.

SONG XXXIII.

BY MRS COCKBURN.

Tune—"The Flowers of the Forest." *

I 'VE seen the smiling
Of Fortune beguiling,
I 've felt all its favours, and found its decay;
Sweet was its blessing,
Kind its caressing,
But now 'tis fled,—fled far away.

I 've seen the forest
Adorned the foremost,
With flowers of the fairest, most pleasant and gay;
Sae bonny was their blooming,
Their scent the air perfuming;
But now they are wither'd and weeded away.

* See before, p. 347. This song is suspected to allude to the consequences of 1715 or 1745.

I've seen the morning
With gold the hills adorning,
And loud tempest storming before the mid-day.
I've seen Tweed's silver streams
Shining in the sunny beams,
Grow drumly and dark as he row'd on his way.

O fickle Fortune !
Why this cruel sporting ?
O why still perplex us, poor sons of a day !
Nae mair your smiles can cheer me,
Nae mair your frowns can fear me,
For the flowers of the forest are wither'd away.

SONG XXXIV.

TO DAUNTON ME.

To daun - ton me, to daun - ton me, Do you ken the thing that would daun - ton me? Eight - y - eight, and eight - y - nine, And a' the drear - y years

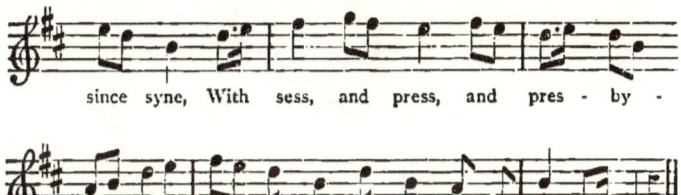

since syne, With sess, and press, and pres-by-try, Good faith, this had li-ken till a daun-ton me.

But to wanton me, but to wanton me,
Do you ken the thing that would wanton me?
To see gude corn upon the rigs,
And banishment to all the Whigs,
And right restored where right should be;
Oh! these are the things that would wanton me.

But to wanton me, but to wanton me,
And ken ye what maist would wanton me?
To see King James at Edinb'rough cross,
With fifty thousand foot and horse,
And the usurper forced to flee;
Oh! this is what maist would wanton me.

SONG XXXIV.*

YE JACOBITES BY NAME.

SAID TO BE BY ROBERT BURNS, FOUNDED ON SOME OLD FRAGMENTS.

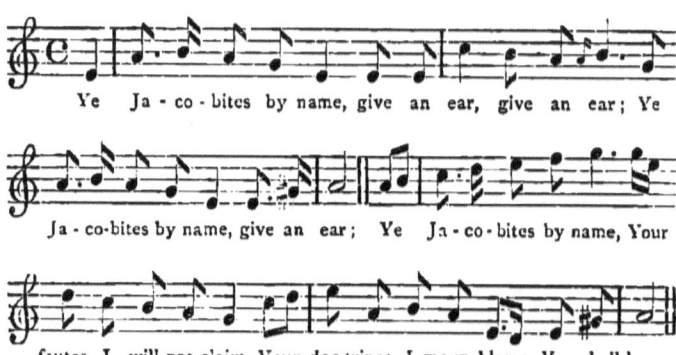

Ye Ja-co-bites by name, give an ear, give an ear; Ye Ja-co-bites by name, give an ear; Ye Ja-co-bites by name, Your fautes I will pro-claim, Your doc-trines I maun blame, You shall hear.

What is right, and what is wrang, by the law, by the law?
What is right, and what is wrang, by the law?
    What is right, and what is wrang?
    A short sword, and a lang,
    A weak arm, and a strang
        For to draw.

What makes heroic strife, famed afar, famed afar?
What makes heroic strife, famed afar?
    What makes heroic strife?
    To whet th' assassin's knife,
    Or hunt a parent's life
        Wi' bludie war.

SCOTISH SONGS.

Then let your schemes alone, in the state, in the state;
Then let your schemes alone, in the state;
    Then let your schemes alone,
    Adore the rising sun,
    And leave a man undone
    To his fate.

SONG XXXIV.**

ORAN AN AOIG, OR, THE SONG OF DEATH.

BY ROBERT BURNS.

A Gaelic Air.

Fare-well, thou fair day, thou green earth and ye skies, Now gay with the broad set-ting sun! Fare-well, loves and friend-ships, ye dear ten-der ties! Our race of ex-ist-ence is run. Thou grim king of ter-rors, thou life's gloom-y foe, Go fright-en

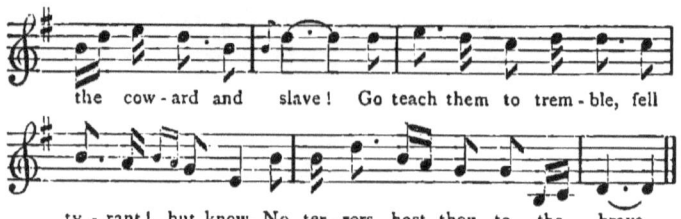

Thou strik'st the dull peasant, he sinks in the dark,
    Nor saves e'en the wreck of a name :
Thou strik'st the young hero, a glorious mark !
    He falls in the blaze of his fame.
In the field of proud honour, our swords in our hands,
    Our king and our country to save,
While victory shines on life's last ebbing sands,
    Oh, who would not die with the brave?

SONG XXXV.

MACPHERSON'S LAMENT.*

* A noted Freebooter, natural son of a Highland gentleman, by a gipsy. He was executed at the cross of Banff, November 16, 1700. He played the above tune upon a favourite violin at the gallows, offered it to any of his clan who would undertake to play the tune over his body, at his lyke waik; as none answered, he dashed the instrument to pieces over the executioner's head, and flung himself from the ladder.

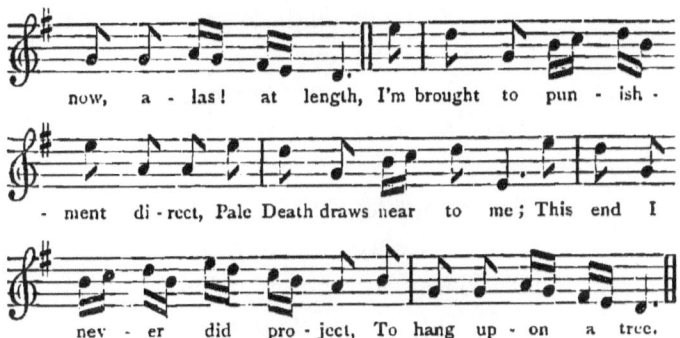

To hang upon a tree! a tree!
  That cursed unhappy death!
Like to a wolf to worried be,
  And choaked in the breath.
My very heart would surely break,
  When this I think upon,
Did not my courage singular
  Bid pensive thoughts begone.

No man on earth that draweth breath
  More courage had than I;
I dared my foes unto their face,
  And would not from them fly:
This grandeur stout, I did keep out,
  Like Hector manfullie;
Then wonder one like me, so stout,
  Should hang upon a tree.

Th' Egyptian band I did command,
  With courage more by far
Than ever did a general
  His soldiers in a war:

Being fear'd by all, both great and small,
    I lived most joyfullie;
Oh! curse upon this fate of mine,
    To hang upon a tree!

As for my life, I do not care,
    If justice would take place,
And bring my fellow-plunderers
    Unto this same disgrace;
For Peter Brown, that notour loon,
    Escaped, and was made free:
Oh! curse upon this fate of mine,
    To hang upon a tree!

Both law and justice buried are,
    And fraud and guile succeed,
The guilty pass unpunished,
    If money intercede:
The laird of Grant, that Highland saint,
    His mighty majestie,
He pleads the cause of Peter Brown,
    And lets Macpherson die.

The dest'ny of my life contrived
    By those whom I obliged,
Rewarded me much ill for good,
    And left me no refuge:
For Braco Duff, in rage enough,
    He first laid hands on me;
And if that death would not prevent
    Avenged would I be.

As for my life, it is but short,
　　When I shall be no more;
To part with life I am content,
　　As any heretofore.
Therefore, good people all, take heed,
　　This warning take by me,
According to the lives you lead,
　　Rewarded you will be.

SONG XXXVI.

MACPHERSON'S FAREWELL.

BY ROBERT BURNS.

Tune—"Macpherson's Lament." *

Farewell, ye dungeons dark and strong,
　　The wretch's destinie!
Macpherson's time will not be long,
　　On yonder gallows tree.
　　　　Sae rantingly, sae wantonly,
　　　　　　Sae dauntingly gaed he,
　　　　He play'd a spring, and danced it round,
　　　　　　Below the gallows tree.

Oh, what is death but parting breath?
　　On mony a bloody plain
I've dared his face, and in this place
　　I scorn him yet again.
　　　　Sae rantingly, &c.

* See page 454.

Untie these bands from off my hands,
   And bring me to my sword,
And there's no man in all Scotland
   But I'll brave at a word.
        Sae rantingly, &c.

I've lived a life of sturt and strife;
   I die by treacherie:
It burns my heart I must depart,
   And not avenged be.
        Sae rantingly, &c.

Now farewell light, thou sunshine bright.
   And all beneath the sky!
May coward shame disdain his name,
   The wretch that dares not die!
        Sae rantingly, &c.

SONG XXXVII.

LEADER HAUGHS AND YARROW.

BY NICOL BURNE.

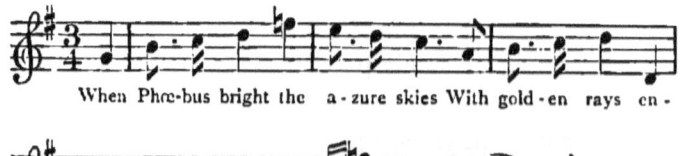

When Phœ-bus bright the a-zure skies With gold-en rays en-light-neth, He makes all Na-ture's beau-ties rise, Herbs, trees, and

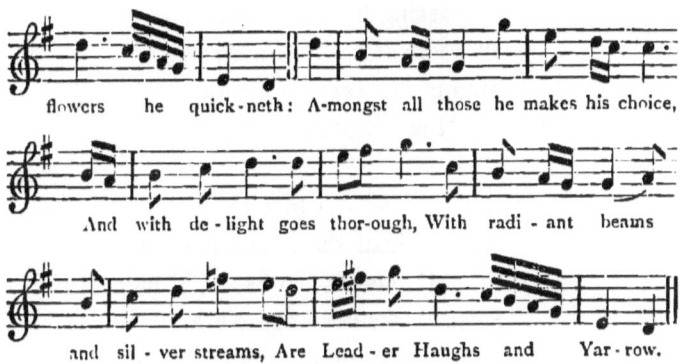

When Aries the day and night
    In equal length divideth,
Auld frosty Saturn takes his flight,
    Nae langer he abideth:
Then Flora queen, with mantle green,
    Casts aff her former sorrow,
And vows to dwell with Ceres sell,
    In Leader Haughs and Yarrow.

Pan playing on his aiten reed,
    And shepherds him attending,
Do here resort their flocks to feed,
    The hills and haughs commending;
With cur and kent upon the bent,
    Sing to the sun good-morrow,
And swear nae fields mair pleasures yield,
    Than Leader Haughs and Yarrow.

An house there stands on Leader-side,
    Surmounting my descriving,
With rooms sae rare, and windows fair,
    Like Dedalus' contriving;

Men passing by do aften cry,
   In sooth it hath no marrow;
It stands as sweet on Leader-side,
   As Newark does on Yarrow.

A mile below wha lists to ride,
   They'll hear the mavis singing;
Into St Leonard's banks she'll bide,
   Sweet birks her head o'erhinging:
The lintwhite loud and Progne proud,
   With tuneful throats and narrow,
Into St Leonard's banks they sing,
   As sweetly as in Yarrow.

The lapwing lilteth o'er the lee,
   With nimble wing she sporteth;
But vows she'll flee far from the tree
   Where Philomel resorteth:
By break of day the lark can say
   I'll bid you a good-morrow,
I'll stretch my wing and mounting sing,
   O'er Leader Haughs and Yarrow.

Park, Wanton-waws, and Wooden-cleugh,
   The East and Western Mainses,
The wood of Lauder's fair enough,
   The corns are good in Blainshes;
Where aits are fine, and sald by kind,
   That if ye search all thorough,
Mearns, Buchan, Mar, nane better are
   Than Leader Haughs and Yarrow.

In Burnmill-bog, and Whitslade shaws,
    The fearful hare she haunteth;
Brig-haugh and Braidwoodsheil she knaws,
    And Chapel-wood frequenteth:
Yet when she irks, to Kaidsly birks
    She rins, and sighs for sorrow,
That she should leave sweet Leader Haughs,
    And cannot win to Yarrow.

What sweeter musick wad ye hear,
    Than hounds and beigles crying?
The started hare rins hard with fear,
    Upon her speed relying:
But yet her strength it fails at length,
    Nae bielding can she borrow
In Sorrel's fields, Cleckman, or Hags,
    And sighs to be in Yarrow.

For Rockwood, Ringwood, Spoty, Shag,
    With sight and scent pursue her,
Till, ah! her pith begins to flag,
    Nae cunning can rescue her:
O'er dub and dyke, o'er seugh and syke,
    She'll rin the fields all thorough,
Till fail'd she fa's in Leader Haughs,
    And bids fareweel to Yarrow.

Sing Erslington and Cowdenknows,
    Where Homes had anes commanding;
And Drygrange with the milk-white ewes,
    'Twixt Tweed and Leader standing:

The bird that flees through Reedpath trees,
 And Gledswood banks ilk morrow,
May chant and sing sweet Leader Haughs,
 And bonny howms of Yarrow.

But Minstrel-burn cannot assuage
 His grief while life endureth,
To see the changes of this age,
 That fleeting time procureth:
For mony a place stands in hard case,
 Where blyth fowk kend nae sorrow,
With Homes that dwelt on Leader-side,
 And Scots that dwelt on Yarrow.

———◆———

SONG XXXVIII.

Tune—"Gillicrankie." *

When Guilford good our pilot stood,
 An' did our hellim thraw, man,
Ae night, at tea, began a plea,
 Within America, man:
Then up they gat the maskin-pat,
 And in the sea did jaw, man;
An' did nae less, in full Congress,
 Than quite refuse our law, man.

---

* See before, p. 385. The events and allusions which form the subject of this song, are too recent and familiar to need a comment.

Then through the lakes Montgomery takes,
    I wat he was na slaw, man ;
Down Lowrie's burn he took a turn,
    And Carleton did ca', man :
But yet, whatreck, he, at Quebec,
    Montgomery-like did fa', man,
Wi' sword in hand, before his band,
    Amang his en'mies a', man.

Poor Tammy Gage, within a cage
    Was kept in Boston-ha', man ;
Till Willie Howe took o'er the knowe
    For Philadelphia, man :
Wi' sword an' gun he thought a sin
    Guid Christian bluid to draw, man ;
But at New York, wi' knife an' fork,
    Sir Loin he hashed sma', man.

Burgoyne gaed up, like spur an' whip,
    Till Fraser brave did fa', man ;
Then lost his way, ae misty day,
    In Saratoga shaw, man.
Cornwallis fought as lang's he dought,
    An' did the buckskins claw, man ;
But Clinton's glaive fra rust to save,
    He hung it to the wa', man.

Then Montague, an' Guilford too,
    Began to fear a fa', man ;
And Sackville doure, wha stood the stoure,
    The German chief to thraw, man :

For Paddy Burke, like ony Turk,
    Nae mercy had at a', man;
An' Charlie Fox threw by the box,
    An' lowsed his tinkler jaw, man.

Then Rockingham took up the game,
    Till Death did on him ca', man;
When Shelburne meek held up his cheek,
    Conform to gospel law, man:
Saint Stephen's boys, wi' jarring noise,
    They did his measures thraw, man:
For North an' Fox united stocks,
    An' bore him to the wa', man.

Then clubs an' hearts were Charlie's cartes,
    He swept the stakes awa', man,
Till the diamond's ace, of Indian race,
    Led him a fair *faux pas*, man:
The Saxon lads, wi' loud placads,
    On Chatham's boy did ca', man;
An' Scotland drew her pipe an' blew,
    "Up, Willie, war them a', man!"

Behind the throne then Grenville's gone,
    A secret word or twa, man;
While slee Dundas aroused the class
    Be-north the Roman wa', man:
An' Chatham's wraith, in heavenly graith,
    (Inspired bardies saw, man,)
Wi' kindling eyes cried, "Willie, rise!
    Would I hae fear'd them a', man!"

But, word an' blow, North, Fox, and Co.
  Gowff'd Willie like a ba', man,
'Till Suthron raise, an' coost their claise
  Behind him in a raw, man :
An' Caledon threw by the drone,
  An' did her whittle draw man ;
An' swoor fu' rude, through dirt and blood,
  To mak it guid in law, man.

SONG XXXIX.

BY JAMES THOMSON, ESQ.*

When Bri-tain first, at Heaven's com-mand, A-
rose from out the a-zure main;
A-rose, A-rose from out the a-zure main;
This was the char-ter, the char-ter of the land, And

* In the Masque of Alfred.

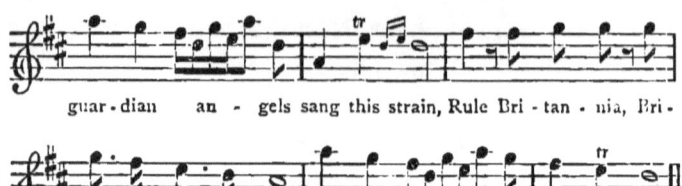

guar-dian an - gels sang this strain, Rule Britan-nia, Britan-nia, rule the waves; Britons nev - er will be slaves.

  The nations, not so blest as thee,
   Must, in their turn, to tyrants fall:
  While thou shalt flourish great and free,
   The dread and envy of them all.
     Rule, &c.

  Still more majestic shalt thou rise,
   More dreadful, from each foreign stroke:
  As the loud blast that tears the skies,
   Serves but to root thy native oak.
     Rule, &c.

  Thee haughty tyrants ne'er shall tame:
   All their attempts to bend thee down,
  Will but arouse thy generous flame;
   But work their woe, and thy renown.
     Rule, &c.

  To thee belongs the rural reign;
   Thy cities shall with commerce shine:
  All thine shall be the subject main,
   And every shore it circles thine.
     Rule, &c.

The muses, still with freedom found,
　　Shall to thy happy coast repair;
Blest isle! with matchless beauty crown'd,
　　And manly hearts to guard the fair.
　　　　Rule, Britannia, Britannia, rule the waves;
　　　　Britons never will be slaves.

SONG XI.

THE DEATH SONG OF THE CHEROKEE INDIANS.*

BY MRS HUNTER.

The sun sets in night, and the stars shun the day,

But glo - ry re - mains when their lights fade a - way; Be -

* "The simple melody" of this song, as we are informed by its fair author, "was brought to England ten years ago by a gentleman named Turner, who had (owing to some singular events in his life) spent nine years amongst the natives of America; he assured the author," she continues, "that it was peculiar to that tribe or nation called the Cherokees, and that they chanted it to a barbarous jargon, implying contempt for their enemies, in the moments of torture and death." She adds, that "the words have been thought something characteristic of the spirit and sentiments of those brave savages;" that "we look upon the fierce and stubborn courage of the dying Indian with a mixture of respect, pity, and horror; and" that "it is to those sentiments in the breast of the hearer that the death song must owe its effect."

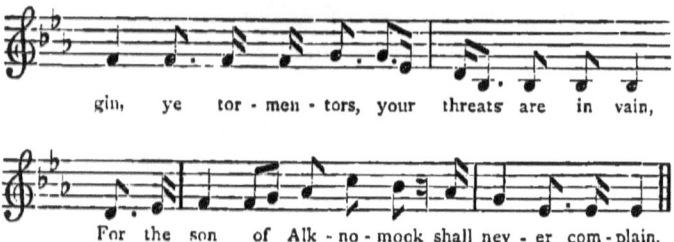

gin, ye tor-men-tors, your threats are in vain,
For the son of Alk-no-mook shall nev-er com-plain.

Remember the arrows he shot from his bow,
Remember your chiefs by his hatchet laid low :
Why so slow ? Do you wait till I shrink from the pain ?
No, the son of Alknomook will never complain.

Remember the wood where in ambush we lay,
And the scalps which we bore from your nation away ;
Now the flame rises fast, you exult in my pain,
But the son of Alknomook can never complain.

I go to the land where my father is gone,
His ghost shall rejoice in the fame of his son :
Death comes like a friend, he relieves me from pain ;
And thy son, O Alknomook, has scorn'd to complain.

CLASS THE FOURTH.

SONG I.

THE HEIR OF LINNE.

PART THE FIRST.

LITHE and listen, gentlemen,
   To sing a song I will beginne :
It is of a lord of faire Scotland,
   Which was the unthrifty heire of Linne.

His father was a right good lord,
   His mother a lady of high degree ;
But they, alas ! were dead, him froe,
   And he loved keeping companie.

To spend the daye with merry cheare,
   To drinke and revell every night,
To card and dice from eve to morne,
   It was, I ween, his heart's delighte.

To ride, to runne, to rant, to roare,
   To alwaye spend and never spare,
I wott, an it were the king himselfe,
   Of gold and fee he mote be bare.

Soe fares the unthrifty lord of Linne,
   Till all his gold is gone and spent;
And he mun sell his landes so broad,
   His house, and landes, and all his rent.

His father had a keen stewarde,
   And John o' the Scales was called hee:
But John is become a gentel-man,
   And John has gott both gold and fee.

Sayes, Welcome, welcome, lord of Linne,
   Let nought disturb thy merry cheere,
If thou wilt sell thy landes soe broad,
   Good store of gold Ile give thee heere.

My gold is gone, my money is spent;
   My lande now take it unto thee:
Give me the golde, good John o' the Scales,
   And thine for aye my lande shall bee.

Then John he did him to record draw,
   And John he gave him a gods-pennee;
But for every pound that John agreed,
   The lande, I wis, was well worth three.

He told him the gold upon the borde,
  He was right glad his lande to winne:
The lande is mine, the gold is thine,
  And now Ile be the lord of Linne.

Thus he hath sold his lande soe broad,
  Both hill and holt, and moore and fenne,
All but a poore and lonesome lodge,
  That stood far off in a lonely glenne.

For soe he to his father hight:
  My sonne, whenne I am gonne, sayd he,
Then thou wilt spend thy lande soe broad,
  And thou wilt spend thy gold soe free:

But sweare me nowe upon the roode,
  That lonesome lodge thou 'lt never spend;
For when all the world doth frown on thee,
  Thou there shalt find a faithful friend.

The heire of Linne is full of golde:
  And come with me, my friends, sayd hee,
Let's drinke, and rant, and merry make,
  And he that spares, ne'er mote he thee.

They ranted, drank, and merry made,
  Till all his gold it waxed thinne;
And then his friendes they slunk away;
  They left the unthrifty heire of Linne.

He had never a penny left in his purse,
    Never a penny left but three ;
The tane was brass, the tither was lead,
    And the third it was the white money.

Nowe well-away, sayd the heire of Linne,
    Nowe well-away, and woe is mee,
For when I was the lord of Linne,
    I never wanted gold or fee.

But many a trusty friend have I,
    And why shold I feel dole or care?
Ile borrow of them all by turnes,
    So need I not be never bare.

But one, I wis, was not at home,
    Another had payd his gold away ;
Another called him thriftless loone,
    And bade him sharpely wend his way.

Now well-away, sayd the heire of Linne,
    Now well-away, and woe is me !
For when I had my landes so broad,
    On me they lived right merrilee.

To beg my bread from door to door,
    I wis, it were a brenning shame :
To rob and steal it were a sinne :
    To work my limbs I cannot frame.

Now Ile away to [the] lonesome lodge,
  For there my father bade me wend :
When all the world should frown on me,
  I there shold find a trusty friend.

PART THE SECOND.

Away then hyed the heire of Linne
  O'er hill and holt, and moor and fenne,
Untill he came to [the] lonesome lodge,
  That stood so lowe in a lonely glenne.

He looked up, he looked downe,
  In hope some comfort for to winne,
But bare and lothly were the walles :
  Here's sorry cheare, quo' the heire of Linne.

The little windowe dim and darke
  Was hung with ivy, brere, and yewe ;
No shimmering sunn here ever shone ;
  No halesome breeze here ever blew.

No chair, ne table he mote spye,
  No chearful hearth, ne welcome bed,
Nought save a rope with renning noose,
  That dangling hung up o'er his head.

And over it in broad letters,
  These words were written so plain to see :
"Ah! graceless wretch, hath spent thine all,
  And brought thyselfe to penurie ?

"All this my boding mind misgave,
  I therefore left this trusty friend:
Let it now sheeld thy foule disgrace,
  And all thy shame and sorrows end."

Sorely shent with this rebuke,
  Sorely shent was the heire of Linne,
His heart, I wis, was near to brast,
  With guilt and sorrowe, shame and sinne.

Never a word spake the heire of Linne,
  Never a word he spake but three:
"This is a trusty friend indeed,
  And is right welcome unto mee."

Then round his necke the corde he drewe,
  And sprang aloft with his bodie:
When lo! the ceiling burst in twaine,
  And to the ground came tumbling hee.

Astonyed lay the heire of Linne,
  Ne knew if he were live or dead,
At length he look'd, and saw a bille,
  And in it a key of gold so redd.

He took the bill, and lookt it on,
  Strait good comfort found he there:
It told him of a hole in the wall,
  In which there stood three chests in-sere.

Two were full of the beaten golde,
    The third was full of white money;
And over them in broad letters
    These words were written soe plaine to see:

"Once more, my sonne, I sette thee cleare,
    Amend thy life and follies past;
For but thou amend thee of thy life,
    That rope must be thy end at last."

And let it bee, sayd the heire of Linne;
    And let it bee, but if I amend:
For here I will make mine avow,
    This reade shall guide me to the end.

Away then went the heire of Linne,
    Away he went with a merry cheare;
I wis, he neither stint ne stayd,
    Till John o' the Scales' house he came neare.

And when he came to John o' the Scales,
    Up at the speere then looked hee;
There sate three lordes at the bordes end,
    Were drinking of the wine so free.

And then bespake the heire of Linne,
    To John o' the Scales then louted hee,
"I pray thee now, good John o' the Scales
    One forty pence for to lend me."

"Away, away, thou thriftless loone;
　Away, away, this may not bee:
For Christ's curse on my head," he sayd,
　"If ever I trust thee one pennie."

Then bespake the heire of Linne,
　To John o' the Scales' wife then spake hee:
"Madame, some almes on me bestowe,
　I pray for sweet saint Charitie."

"Away, away, thou thriftless loone,
　I swear thou gettest no almes of mee;
For if we shold hang any losel heere,
　The first we wold begin with thee."

Then bespake a good fellowe,
　Which sat at John o' the Scales his bord:
Sayd, "Turn againe, thou heire of Linne;
　Some time thou wast a well good lord:

"Some time a good fellow thou hast been,
　And sparedst not thy gold and fee,
Therefore Ile lend thee forty pence,
　And other forty if need bee.

"And ever, I pray thee, John o' the Scales,
　To let him sit in thy companee:
For well I wot thou hadst his land,
　And a good bargain it was to thee."

Up then spake him John o' the Scales,
    All wood he answer'd him againe.
"Now Christ's curse on my head," he sayd,
    "But I did lose by that bargaine.

"And here I proffer thee, heire of Linne,
    Before these lords so faire and free,
Thou shalt have it backe again better cheape,
    By a hundred markes, than I had it of thee."

"I drawe you to record, lords," he sayd.
    With that he gave him a gods-pennee:
"Now by my fay," sayd the heire of Linne,
    "And here, good John, is thy money."

And he pull'd forth the bagges of gold,
    And layd them down upon the bord:
All woe begone was John o' the Scales,
    Soe shent he cold say never a word.

He told him forth the good red gold,
    He told it forth with mickle dinne.
"The gold is thine the land is mine,
    And now Ime againe the lord of Linne."

Sayes, "Have thou here, thou good fellowe,
    Forty pence thou didst lend mee:
Now I am againe the lord of Linne,
    And forty pounds I will give thee."

SCOTISH SONGS.

"Now well-aday!" sayth Joan o' the Scales:
"Now well-aday! and woe is my life!
Yesterday I was lady of Linne,
Now Ime but John o' the Scales his wife."

"Now fare thee well," sayd the heire of Linne,
"Farewell, good John o' the Scales," said hee:
"When next I want to sell my land,
Good John o' the Scales, Ile come to thee."

SONG II.

THE WEE WEE MAN.

As I was walk-ing all a-lone, be-tween a wa-ter and a wa', And there I spyed a wee wee man, And he was the least that ere I saw. His legs were scarce a shath-mont's length, And thick

and thim-ber was his thighs, Be-tween his brows there was a span, And be-tween his shoul-ders there was three.

He took up a meikle stane,
    And he flang't as far as I could see;
Though I had been as Wallace wight,
    I couldna liften't to my knee.

O wee wee man, but thou be strong;
    O tell me where thy dwelling be?
My dwelling's down at yon bonny bower:
    O will you go with me and see?

On we lap and awa' we rade,
    Till we came to yon bonny green;
We 'lighted down for to bait our horse,
    And out there came a lady fine.

Four-and-twenty at her back,
    And they were a' clad out in green;
Though the king of Scotland had been there,
    The warst o' them might ha' been his queen.

On we lap and awa' we rade,
    Till we came to yon bonny ha',
Where the roof was o' the beaten gould,
    And the floor was o' the crystal a'.

When we came to the stair foot,
 Ladies were dancing jimp and sma';
But, in the twinkling of an eye,
 My wee wee man was clean awa'.

SONG III.

EDWARD, EDWARD.

Quhy dois zour brand sae drop wi' bluid,
 Edward, Edward?
Quhy dois zour brand sae drop wi' bluid?
 And quhy sae sad gang zee, O?
O, I hae kill'd my hauke sae guid,
 Mither, mither:
O, I hae kill'd my hauke sae guid:
 And I hae nae mair bot hee, O.

Zour haukis bluid was nevir sae reid,
 Edward, Edward:
Zour haukis bluid was nevir sae reid,
 My deir son, I tell thee, O.
O, I hae kill'd my reid-roan steid,
 Mither, mither:
O, I hae kill'd my reid-roan steid,
 That erst was sae fair and free, O.

Zour steid was auld, and ze hae gat mair;
 Edward, Edward:
Zour steid was auld, and ze hae gat mair,
 Sum other dule ze drie, O.

O, I hae kill'd my fadir deir,
　　　　　　Mither, mither:
O, I hae kill'd my fadir deir,
　　　Alas! and wae is mee, O!

And quhatten penance wul ze drie for that,
　　　　　　Edward, Edward?
And quhatten penance wul ze drie for that?
　　　My deir son, now tell me, O.
Ile set my feit in zonder boat,
　　　　　　Mither, mither:
Ile set my feit in zonder boat,
　　　And Ile fare ovir the sea, O.

And quhat wul ze do wi' zour towirs and zour ha',
　　　　　　Edward, Edward?
And quhat wul ze do wi' zour towirs and zour ha',
　　　That were sae fair to see, O?
Ile let thame stand till they doun fa',
　　　　　　Mither, mither:
Ile let thame stand till they doun fa',
　　　For here nevir mair maun I bee, O.

And quhat wul ze leive to zour bairns and zour wife,
　　　　　　Edward, Edward?
And quhat wul ze leive to zour bairns and zour wife,
　　　Quhan ze gang ovir the sea, O?
The warldis room, let them beg throw life,
　　　　　　Mither, mither:
The warldis room, let them beg throw life,
　　　For thame nevir mair wul I see, O.

And quhat wul ze leive to zour ain mither deir,
                    Edward, Edward!
And quhat wul ze leive to zour ain mither deir?
        My deir son, now tell me, O.
The curse of hell frae me sall ze beir,
                    Mither, mither:
The curse of hell frae me sall ze beir,
        Sic counseils ze gave to me, O.

SONG IV.

HARDYKNUTE.*

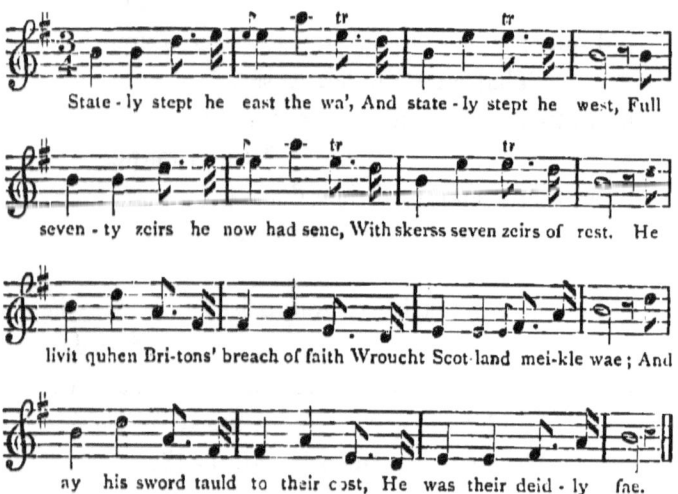

* "A [pretended] fragment," written in or about 1718. See the "Historical Essay," page 57.

Hie on a hill his castle stude,
  With halls and touris a hicht,
And guidly chambers fair to se,
  Quhair he lodgit mony a knicht.
His dame sae peirless anes and fair,
  For chast and bewtie deimt,
Nae marrow had in all the land,
  Saif Elenor the quene.

Full thirtein sons to him scho bare,
  All men of valour stout;
In bluidy ficht with sword in hand
  Nyne lost their lives bot doubt;
Four zit remain, lang may they live
  To stand by liege and land!
Hie was their fame, hie was their micht,
  And hie was their command.

Great luve they bare to Fairly fair,
  Their sister saft and deir;
Her girdle shawd her middle gimp,
  And gowden glist her hair.
Quhat waefou wae hir bewtie bred!
  Waefou to zung and auld,
Waefou I trow to kyth and kin,
  As story ever tauld.

The king of Norse in summer tyde,
  Puft up with powir and micht,
Landed in fair Scotland the yle,
  With many a hardy knicht:

The tydings to our gude Scots king
    Came, as he sat at dyne,
With noble chiefs in braif aray,
    Drinking the blude-reid wyne.

" To horse, to horse, my ryal liege,
    Zour faes stand on the strand,
Full twenty thousand glittering spears
    The king of Norse commands."
Bring me my steed Mage dapple gray,
    Our gude king raise and cryd,
A trustier beast in all the land
    A Scots king never seyd.

Go, little page, tell Hardyknute,
    That lives on hill so hie,
To draw his sword, the dreid of foes,
    And haste and follow me.
The little page flew swift as dart
    Flung by his master's arm;
" Cum down, cum down, Lord Hardyknute,
    And rid zour king frae harm."

Then reid, reid grew his dark-brown cheiks
    Sae did his dark-brown brow;
His luiks grew kene, as they were wont
    In dangers great to do;
He hes tane a horn as grene as glass,
    And gein five sounds sae shrill,
That treis in grene wod schuke thereat,
    Sae loud rang ilka hill.

His sons in manly sport and glie,
  Had past that summer's morn,
Quhen, lo, down in a grassy dale,
  They heard their fatheris horn.
"That horn," quod they, "neir sounds in peace,
  We haif other sport to byde;"
And sune they heyd them up the hill,
  And sune were at his syde.

"Late late zestrene I weind in peace
  To end my lengthned lyfe,
My age micht weil excuse my arm
  Frae manly feats of stryfe;
But now that Norse dois proudly boast
  Fair Scotland to inthrall,
Its neir be said of Hardyknute,
  He feard to ficht or fall.

"Robin of Rothsay, bend thy bow,
  Thy arrows schute sae leil,
Mony a comely countenance
  They haif turnd to deidly pale:
Brade Thomas, tak ze but zour lance,
  Ze neid nae weapons mair,
Gif ze ficht weit as ze did anes
  Gainst Westmorland's ferss heir.

"Malcom, licht of fute as stag
  That runs in forest wyld,
Get me my thousands thrie of men
  Well bred to sword and schield:

Bring me my horse and harnisine,
    My blade of mettal cleir."
If faes kend but the hand it bare,
    They sune had fled for feir.

" Fareweil my dame sae peirless gude,"
    And tuke hir by the hand,
" Fairer to me in age zou seim,
    Than maids for bewtie famd:
My zoungest son sall here remain
    To guard these stately towirs,
And shut the silver bolt that keips
    Sae fast zour painted bowirs."

And first scho wet hir comely cheiks,
    And thin hir boddice grene,
Hir silken cords of twirtle twist,
    Weil plett with silver schene;
And apron set with mony a dice
    Of neidle-wark sae rare,
Wove by nae hand, as ze may guess,
    Saif that of Fairly fair.

And he has ridden owre muir and moss,
    Owre hills and mony a glen,
Quhen he came to a wounded knicht,
    Making a heavy mane:
" Here maun I lye, here maun I dye,
    By treacheries false gyles;
Witless I was that eir gaif faith
    To wicked womans smyles."

"Sir knicht, gin ze were in my bowir,
  To lean on silken seat,
My ladyis kyndlie care zoud prove,
  Quha neir kend deidly hate;
Hirself wald watch ze all the day,
  Hir maids a deid of nicht;
And Fairly fair zour heart wald cheir,
  As scho stands in zour sicht.

"Aryse, zoung knicht, and mount zour steid,
  Full lowns the schynand day;
Cheis frae my menzie quhom ze pleis
  To lead ze on the way."
With smyless luke and visage wan,
  The wounded knicht replyd,
Kynd chiftain, zour intent pursue,
  For heir I maun abyde.

To me nae after day nor nicht,
  Can eir be sweit or fair,
But sune, beneath sum draping trie,
  Cauld deith sall end my care.
With him nae pleiding micht prevail,
  Braif Hardyknute to gain,
With fairest words and reason strang,
  Straif courteously in vain.

Syne he has gane far hynd attowre
  Lord Chattan's land sae wyde,
That lord a worthy wicht was ay,
  Quhen faes his courage seyd:

Of Pictish race, by mother's syde,
    When Picts ruld Caledon,
Lord Chattan claimd the princely maid,
    Quhen he saift Pictish crown.

Now with his ferss and stalwart train,
    He reicht a rysing heicht,
Quhair braid encampit on the dale,
    Norse army lay in sicht.
" Zonder, my valziant sons and feris,
    Our raging revers wait,
On the unconquerit Scotish swaird
    To try us with thair fate.

" Mak orisons to him that saift
    Our sauls upon the rude.
Syne braifly schaw zour veins are fill'd
    With Caledonian blude."
Then furth he drew his trusty glaive,
    Quhyle thousands all around,
Drawn frae their sheaths glanst in the sun,
    And loud the bougills sound.

To join his king adoun the hill
    In hast his merch he made,
Quhyle, playand pibrochs, minstralls meit
    Afore him stately strade.
" Thryse welcom, valziant stoup of weir,
    Thy nation's scheild and pryde ;
Thy king nae reason has to feir
    Quhen thou art be his syde."

Quhen bows were bent and darts were thrawn,
    For thrang scarce could they flie,
The darts clove arrows as they met,
    The arrows dart the trie.
Lang did they rage and ficht full ferss,
    With little skaith to man,
But bludy, bludy was the field,
    Or that lang day was done.

The king of Scots that sindle bruik'd
    The war that luikt lyke play,
Drew his braid sword, and brake his bow,
    Sen bows seimt but delay:
Quoth noble Rothsay, Myne I'll keip,
    I wate its bleid a skore.
Hast up my merry men, cryd the king,
    As he rade on before.

The king of Norse he socht to find,
    With him to mense the faucht,
But on his forehead there did licht
    A sharp unsonsie shaft;
As he his hand put up to find
    The wound, an arrow kene,
O waefou chance! there pinn'd his hand
    In midst betwene his ene.

Revenge, revenge, cryd Rothsay's heir,
    Your mail-coat sall nocht byde
The strength and sharpness of my dart;
    Then sent it throuch his syde:

Another arrow weil he markd,
    It persit his neck in twa,
His hands then quat the silver reins,
    He law as eard did fa.

"Sair bleids my leige, sair, sair he bleids."
    Again with micht he drew
And gesture dreid his sturdy bow,
    Fast the braid arrow flew:
Wae to the knicht he ettled at,
    Lament now, quene Elgreid,
Hie, dames, to wail zour darlings fall,
    His zouth and comely meid.

"Take aff, take aff his costly jupe,"
    (Of gold weil was it twynd,
Knit lyke the fowler's net, throuch quhilk
    His steilly harness shynd,)
"Take Norse that gift frae me, and bid
    Him venge the blude it beirs;
Say, if he face my bended bow,
    He sure nae weapon feirs."

Proud Norse, with giant body tall,
    Braid shoulder, and arms strong,
Cryd, Quhair is Hardyknute sae famd,
    And feird at Britain's throne?
Though Britons tremble at his name,
    I sune sall make him wail
That eir my sword was made sae sharp,
    Sae saft his coat of mail.

That brag his stout heart could na byde,
    It lent him zouthfou micht:
I 'm Hardyknute; this day, he cryd,
    To Scotland's king I hecht
To lay thee law as horses hufe;
    My word I mean to keip.
Syne, with the first strake eir he strake,
    He garrd his body bleid.

Norse ene lyke gray gosehawks staird wyld,
    He sicht with shame and spyte:
" Disgracd is now my far famd arm,
    That left thee power to stryke."
Then gaif his head a blaw sae fell,
    It made him doun to stoup
As law as he to ladies usit
    In courtly gyse to lout.

Full sune he raisd his bent body,
    His bow he marvelld fair,
Sen blaws till then on him but darrd
    As touch of Fairly fair:
Norse ferliet too as sair as he
    To se his stately luke,
Sae sune as eir he strake a fae,
    Sae sune his lyfe he tuke.

Quhair, lyke a fyre to hether set,
    Bauld Thomas did advance,
A sturdy fae, with luke enragd,
    Up towards him prance;

He spurd his steid throuch thickest ranks,
    The hardy zouth to quell,
Quha stude unmufit at his approach,
    His furie to repell.

"That schort brown shaft, sae meanly trimd,
    Lukis lyke poor Scotland's geir,
But dreidfull seims the rusty poynt!"
    And loud he leuch in jeir.
"Aft Britain's blude has dimd its shyne,
    This poynt cut short their vaunt:"
Syne piercd the boisteris bairded cheik,
    Nae tyme he tuke to taunt.

Schort quhyle he in his sadill swang,
    His stirrip was nae stay,
Sae feible hang his unbent knee,
    Sure taken he was fey:
Swith on the hardened clay he fell,
    Right far was hard the thud,
But Thomas luikt not as he lay
    All waltering in his blude.

With cairles gesture mynd unmuvit
    On raid he north the plain;
His seim in thrang of fiercest stryfe,
    Quhen winner ay the same:
Nor zit his heart dames dimpelit cheik
    Coud meise saft luve to bruik,
Till vengeful Ann returnd his scorn,
    Then languid grew his luke.

In thrawis of death, with wallowit cheik,
    All panting on the plain,
The fainting corps of warriours lay,
    Neir to aryse again;
Neir to return to native land,
    Nae mair, with blythsom sounds,
To boist the glories of the day,
    And schaw thair shyning wounds.

On Norway's coast the widowit dame
    May wash the rocks with teirs,
May lang luke owre the schiples seis
    Before hir mate appeirs.
Ceise, Emma, ceise to hope in vain,
    Thy lord lyis in the clay,
The valziant Scots nae revers thole
    To carry lyfe away.

There on a lie, quhair stands a cross
    Set up for monument,
Thousands full fierce that summers day
    Fill'd kene waris black intent.
Let Scots, quhyle Scots, praise Hardyknute,
    Let Norse the name ay dreid,
Ay how he faucht, aft how he spaird,
    Sall latest ages reid.

Loud and chill blew [the] westlin wind,
    Sair beat the heavy showir,
Mirk grew the nicht eir Hardyknute
    Wan neir his stately tower;

His towir, that us'd with torches bleise,
    To shyne sae far at nicht,
Seimd now as black as mourning weid,
    Nae marvel sair he sichd.

"Thairs nae licht in my ladys bowir,
    Thairs nae licht in my hall;
Nae blink shines round my Fairly fair,
    Nor ward stands on my wall.
Quhat bodes it? Robert, Thomas, say!"
    Nae answer fits their dreid.
"Stand back, my sons, I'll be zour gyde."—
    But by they past with speid.

"As fast I haif sped owre Scotlands faes"—
    There ceist his brag of weir,
Sair schamit to mynd ocht but his dame,
    And maiden Fairly fair.
Black feir he felt, but quhat to feir
    He wist not zet with dreid;
Sair schuke his body, sair his limbs,
    And all the warrior fled.

SONG V.

GIL MORRICE.*

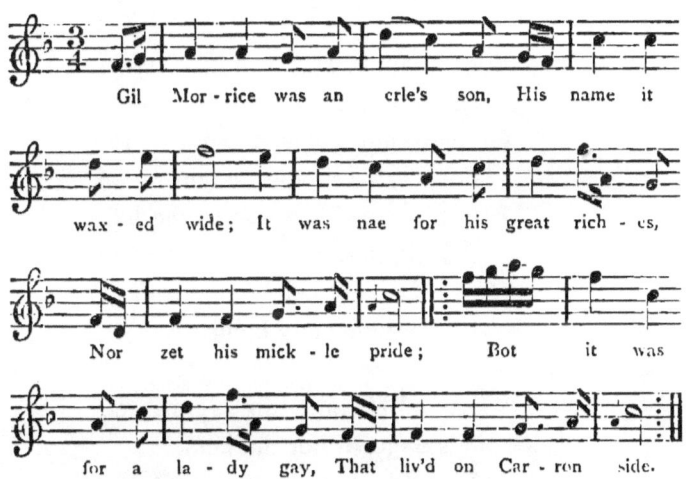

Gil Mor-rice was an erle's son, His name it wax-ed wide; It was nae for his great rich-es, Nor zet his mick-le pride; Bot it was for a la-dy gay, That liv'd on Car-ron side.

"QUHAIR sall I get a bonny boy
  That will win hose and shoen;
That will gae to Lord Barnards ha,
  And bid his lady cum?
And ze maun rin my errand, Willie;
  And ze maun rin wi' pride;
Quhen other boys gae on their foot,
  On horseback ze sall ride."

"Oh no! oh no! my master dear!
  I dare nae for my life;
I'll no gae to the bauld barons,
  For to triest furth his wife."

* See the "Historical Essay," page 57.

My bird Willie, my boy Willie,
    My dear Willie, he said,
How can ze strive against the stream?
    For I sall be obeyd.

But oh, my master dear! he cryd,
    In grene wod ze're zour lain;
Gi owre sic thochts, I walde ze rede,
    For fear ze should be tain.
Haste, haste, I say, gae to the ha',
    Bid hir cum here wi' speid:
If ze refuse my heigh command,
    Ill gar zour body bleid.

"Gar bid hir take this gay mantel,
    'Tis a' gowd bot the hem,
Bid hir cum to the gude grene wode,
    And bring nane bot hir lain:
And there it is, a silken sarke,
    Hir ain hand sewd the sleive;
And bid hir cum to Gil Morice,
    Speir nae bauld barons leave."

"Yes, I will gae zour black errand,
    Though it be to zour cost;
Sen ze by me will nae be warn'd,
    In it ze sall find frost.
The baron he is a man of might,
    He neir could bide to taunt,
As ze will see before it's nicht,
    How sma' ze hae to vaunt.

"And sen I maun zour errand rin
  Sae sair against my will,
I 'se mak a vow, and keip it trow,
  It sall be done for ill."
And quhen he came to broken brigue,
  He bent his bow and swam;
And quhen he came to grass growing,
  Set down his feet and ran.

And quhen he came to Barnard's ha',
  Would neither chap nor ca',
Bot set his bent bow to his breist,
  And lichtly lap the wa'.
He wauld nae tell the man his errand,
  Though he stude at the gait;
Bot straight into the ha' he cam,
  Quhair they were set at meit.

"Hail! hail! my gentle sire and dame!
  My message winna waite;
Dame, ze maun to the gude grene wod
  Before that it be late.
Ze're bidden tak this gay mantel,
  'Tis a' gowd bot the hem:
Zou maun gae to the gude grene wode,
  Ev'n by your sel alane:

"And there it is, a silken sarke,
  Your ain hand sewd the sleive;
Ze maun gae speik to Gil Morice,
  Speir nae bauld barons leave."

The lady stamped wi' her foot,
 And winked wi' her ee;
Bot a' that she could say or do,
 Forbidden he wad nae bee.

" It 's surely to my bow'r-woman;
 It neir could be to me."
" I brocht it to Lord Barnard's lady;
 I trow that ze be she."
Then up and spack the wylie nurse,
 (The bairn upon hir knee,)
" If it be cum frae Gil Morice,
 It 's deir welcum to me."

" Ze leid, ze leid, ze filthy nurse,
 Sae loud I heird ze lee;
I brocht it to Lord Barnard's lady;
 I trow ze be nae shee."
Then up and spack the bauld baron,
 An angry man was hee;
He 's tain the table wi' his foot,
 Sae has he wi' his knee;
Till siller cup and mazer dish
 In flinders he gard flee.

" Gae bring a robe of your cliding,
 That hings upon the pin,
And I 'll gae to the gude grene wode
 And speik wi' zour lemman."

"O bide at hame, now Lord Barnard,
　　I warde ze bide at hame;
Neir wyte a man for violence,
　　That neir wate ze wi' nane."

Gil Morice sate in gude grene wode,
　　He whistled and he sang:
"Oh what mean a' the folk coming?
　　My mother tarries lang."
His hair was like the threeds of gold,
　　Drawne frae Minerva's loome;
His lipps like roses drapping dew,
　　His breath was a' perfume.

His brow was like the mountain snae
　　Gilt by the morning beam;
His cheeks like living roses glow;
　　His een like azure stream.
The boy was clad in robes of grene,
　　Sweete as the infant spring;
And like the mavis on the bush,
　　He gart the vallies ring.

The baron came to the grene wode,
　　Wi' mickle dule and care,
And there he first spied Gil Morice
　　Kameing his zellow hair:
That sweetly waved around his face,
　　That face beyond compare:
He sang sae sweet, it might dispel
　　A' rage but fell despair.

" Nae wonder, nae wonder, Gil Morice,
    My lady loed thee weel,
The fairest part of my bodie
    Is blacker than thy heel.
Zet neir the less now, Gil Morice,
    For a' thy great beautie,
Ze's rew the day ze eir was born,
    That head sall gae wi' me."

Now he has drawn his trusty brand,
    And slaited on the strae;
And through Gil Morice' fair body
    He's "gart" cauld iron gae.
And he has tain Gil Morice' head
    And set it on a speir;
The meanest man in a' his train
    Has gotten that head to bear.

And he has tain Gil Morice up,
    Laid him across his steid,
And brocht him to his painted bowr,
    And laid him on a bed.
The lady sat on castil wa',
    Beheld baith dale and down;
And there she saw Gil Morice' head
    Cum trailing to the toun.

" Far better I loe that bluidy head,
    Bot and that zellow hair,
Than Lord Barnard, and a' his lands,
    As they lig here and thair."

And she has tain her Gil Morice,
    And kiss'd baith mouth and chin :
" I was once as fow of Gil Morice,
    As the hip is o' the stean.

" I got ze in my father's house,
    Wi' mickle sin and shame,
I brocht thee up in gude grene wode,
    Under the heavy rain ;
Oft have I by thy cradle sitten,
    And fondly seen thee sleip ;
But now I gae about thy grave,
    The saut tears for to weip."

And syne she kiss'd his bluidy cheik,
    And syne his bluidy chin :
" O better I loe my Gil Morice
    Than a' my kith and kin ! "
" Away, away, ze ill woman,
    And an il deith mait ze dee :
Gin I had kend he'd bin zour son,
    He'd neir bin slain for mee."

" Obraid me not, my Lord Barnard !
    Obraid me not for shame !
Wi' that saime speir O pierce my heart !
    And put me out o' pain.
Since nothing bot Gil Morice head
    Thy jelous rage could quell,
Let that saim hand now take hir life
    That neir to thee did ill.

"To me nae after days nor nichts
    Will eir be saft and kind;
I'll fill the air with heavy sighs,
    And greet till I am blind."
"Enouch of blood by me's bin spilt,
    Seek not zour death frae mee;
I rather lourd it had been my sel
    Than eather him or thee.

"With waefo wae I hear zour plaint;
    Sair, sair I rew the deid,
That eir this cursed hand of mine
    Had gard his body bleid.
Dry up zour teirs, my winsome dame,
    Ze neir can heal his wound,
Ze see his head upon the speir,
    His heart's blude on the ground.

"I curse the hand that did the deid,
    The heart that thocht the ill;
The feet that bore me wi' sik speid,
    The comely zouth to kill.
I'll ay lament for Gil Morice,
    As gin he were mine ain;
I'll neir forget the dreiry day
    On which the zouth was slain."

SONG VI.

THE YOUNG LAIRD OF OCHILTRIE.*

O LISTEN, gude peopell, to my tale,
Listen to quhat I tel to thee;
The king has taiken a poor prisoner,
The wanton laird of Ochiltrie.

---

* It is not easy to discover to whom or what period this ballad alludes. A Lord Ochiltrie, in 1631, was sentenced to perpetual imprisonment in Blackness Castle, (where he continued twenty years,) for calumniating the Marquis of Hamilton.—Burnet's *Memoirs of James and William Dukes of Hamilton*, p. 13.

It is conjectured that this ballad is founded on the following circumstance which took place in 1592, when Bothwell was carrying on his schemes against the person of James VI. The name of the hero has been changed by reciters from Bogie, as in the story, to Ochiltrie, for what reason has not been discovered:—

"At the same time, John Weymis, younger of Bogie, gentleman of his majesty's chamber, and in great favour both with the king and queen, was discovered to have the like dealing with Bothwell; and being committed to the keeping of the guard, escaped by the policy of one of the Dutch maids, with whom he entertained a secret love. The gentlewoman, named Mistress Margaret Twinslace, coming one night, whilst the king and queen were in bed, to his keepers, showed that the king called for the prisoner, to ask of him some question. The keepers, suspecting nothing, for they knew her to be the principal maid in the chamber, conveighed him to the door of the bed-chamber, and making a stay without, as they were commanded, the gentlewoman did let him down at a window, by a cord that she had prepared. The keepers waiting upon his return, stayed there until the morning, and then found themselves deceived. This, with the manner of the escape, ministered great occasion of laughter; and, not many days after, the king being pacified by the queen's means, he was pardoned, and took to wife the gentlewoman who had, in this sort, hazarded her credit for his safety."—Spotswood's *History*.

Quhen news cam to our guidly queen,
    Sche sicht, and said richt mournfullie,
O quhat will cum of lady Margret,
    Quha beirs sick luve to Ochiltrie?

Lady Margret tore hir yellow hair,
    Quhen as the queen tald hir the saim:
" I wis that I had neir bin born,
    Nor neir had knawn Ochiltrie's naim."

" Fie na," quoth the queen, " that maunna be,
    Fie na, that maunna be;
I'll fynd ze out a better way
    To saif the lyfe of Ochiltrie."

The queen sche trippit up the stair,
    And lawly knielt upon hir knie;
" The first boon quhich I cum to craive
    Is the lyfe of gentel Ochiltrie."

" O iff you had ask'd me castels or towirs,
    I wad hae gin thaim, twa or thrie,
But a' the monie in fair Scotland
    Winna buy the lyfe of Ochiltrie."

The queen sche trippit down the stair,
    And down sche gade richt mournfullie:
" Its a' the monie in fair Scotland
    Winna buy the lyfe of Ochiltrie."

Lady Margret tore hir yellow hair,
    Quhen as the queen tald hir the saim:
" I 'll tak a knife and end my lyfe,
    And be in the grave as soon as him."

" Ah na, fie na," quoth the queen,
    " Fie! na, fie! na, this maunna be;
I 'll set ze on a better way
    To loose and set Ochiltrie frie."

The queen sche slippit up the stair,
    And sche gaid up richt privatlie,
And sche has stoun the prison keys,
    And gane and set Ochiltrie frie.

And sche 's gien him a purse of gowd,
    And another of whyt monie,
Sche 's gien him twa pistoles by 's side,
    Saying to him, " Shute quhen ze win frie."

And quhen he cam to the queen's window,
    Quhaten a joyfou shute gae he!
" Peace be to our royal queen,
    And peace be in hir companie!"

" O quhaten a voyce is that?" quoth the king,
    " Quhaten a voyce is that?" quoth he,
" Quhaten a voyce is that?" quoth the king;
    " I think its the voyce of Ochiltrie.

" Call to me a' my gaolours,
  Call thaim by thirtie and by thrie ;
Quhair for the morn at twelve a clock
  It 's hangit schall they ilk ane be."

" O didna ze send zour keyis to us ?
  Ze sent thaim be thirtie and be thrie ;
And wi thaim sent a strait command,
  To set at lairge zoung Ochiltrie."

" Ah na, fie, na," quoth the queen,
  " Fie, my dear luve, this maunna be ;
And iff ye 're gawn to hang thaim a',
  Indeed ze maun begin wi' me."

The tane was schippit at the pier of Leith,
  The ither at the Queensferrie ;
And now the lady has gotten hir luve,
  The winsom laird of Ochiltrie.

SONG VII.

THE DUKE OF GORDON'S DAUGHTER.*

The Duke of Gor - don has three daugh - ters, E -

- li - za - beth, Mar-garet, and Jean; They would not stay in bon - ny

Cas - tle Gor - don, But they would go to bon - ny A - ber - deen.

They had not been in Aberdeen
A twelvemonth and a day,
Till Lady Jean fell in love with Captain Ogilvie,
And away with him she would gae.

* George (Gordon) fourth Earl of Huntley, who succeeded his grandfather, Earl Alexander, in 1523, and was killed at the battle of Corichie, in 1563, had actually three daughters: Lady Elizabeth, the eldest, married to John Earl of Athole; Lady Margaret, the second, to John Lord Forbes; and Lady Jean, the youngest, to the famous James Earl of Bothwell, from whom being divorced, anno 1568, she married Alexander Earl of Sutherland, who died in 1594, and, surviving him, Alexander Ogilvie of Boyne. The dukedom of Gordon was not created till the year 1684; so that, if the ballad be older, instead of " the Duke of Gordon," the original reading must have been " the Earl of Huntley." As for Alexander Ogilvie, he appears to have succeeded his father, Sir Walter Ogilvie, in the barony of Boyne, about 1560, and to have died in 1606: this Lady Jean being his first wife, by whom he seems to have had no issue.—See Gordon's *History of the Gordons*, and Douglas's *Peerage and Baronage*.

Word came to the Duke of Gordon,
    In the chamber where he lay,
Lady Jean has fell in love with Captain Ogilvie,
    And away with him she would gae.

"Go saddle me the black horse,
    And you'll ride on the grey;
And I will ride to bonny Aberdeen,
    Where I have been many a day."

They were not a mile from Aberdeen,
    A mile but only three,
Till he met with his two daughters walking,
    But away was Lady Jean.

"Where is your sister, maidens?
    Where is your sister, now?
Where is your sister, maidens,
    That she is not walking with you?"

"O pardon us, honour'd father,
    O pardon us, they did say;
Lady Jean is with Captain Ogilvie,
    And away with him she will gae."

When he came to Aberdeen,
    And down upon the green,
There did he see Captain Ogilvie,
    Training up his men.

"O wo to you, Captain Ogilvie,
 And an ill death thou shalt die;
For taking to my daughter,
 Hanged thou shalt be."

Duke Gordon has wrote a broad letter,
 And sent it to the king,
To cause hang Captain Ogilvie,
 If ever he hang'd a man.

"I will not hang Captain Ogilvie,
 For no lord that I see;
But I'll cause him to put off the lace and scarlet,
 And put on the single livery."

Word came to Captain Ogilvie,
 In the chamber where he lay,
To cast off the gold lace and scarlet,
 And put on the single livery.

"If this be for bonny Jeany Gordon,
 This penance I'll take wi';
If this be for bonny Jeany Gordon,
 All this I will dree."

Lady Jean had not been married,
 Not a year but three,
Till she had a babe in every arm,
 Another upon her knee.

"O but I'm weary of wandering!
   O but my fortune is bad!
It sets not the Duke of Gordon's daughter
   To follow a soldier lad.

"O but I'm weary of wandering!
   O but I think lang!
It sets not the Duke of Gordon's daughter
   To follow a single man."

When they came to the Highland hills,
   Cold was the frost and snow;
Lady Jean's shoes they were all torn,
   No farther could she go.

"O! wo to the hills and the mountains!
   Wo to the wind and the rain!
My feet is sore with going barefoot,
   No farther am I able to gang.

"Wo to the hills and the mountains!
   Wo to the frost and the snow!
My feet is sore with going barefoot,
   No farther am I able for to go.

"O! if I were at the glens of Foudlen,
   Where hunting I have been,
I would find the way to bonny Castle-Gordon,
   Without either stockings or shoon."

When she came to Castle-Gordon,
    And down upon the green,
The porter gave out a loud shout,
    "O yonder comes Lady Jean!"

"O you are welcome, bonny Jeany Gordon,
    You are dear welcome to me;
You are welcome, dear Jeany Gordon,
    But away with your Captain Ogilvie."

Now over seas went the captain,
    As a soldier under command;
A message soon follow'd after,
    To come and heir his brother's land.

"Come home, you pretty Captain Ogilvie,
    And heir your brother's land;
Come home, ye pretty Captain Ogilvie,
    Be Earl of Northumberland."

"O! what does this mean?" says the captain,
    "Where's my brother's children three?"
"They are dead and buried,
    And the lands they are ready for thee."

"Then hoist up your sails, brave captain,
    Let's be jovial and free;
I'll to Northumberland, and heir my estate,
    Then my dear Jeany I'll see."

He soon came to Castle-Gordon,
    And down upon the green;
The porter gave out with a loud shout,
    " Here comes Captain Ogilvie!"

" You're welcome, pretty Captain Ogilvie,
    Your fortune's advanced I hear;
No stranger can come unto my gates,
    That I do love so dear."

" Sir, the last time I was at your gates,
    You would not let me in;
I'm come for my wife and children,
    No friendship else I claim."

" Come in, pretty Captain Ogilvie,
    And drink of the beer and the wine;
And thou shalt have gold and silver,
    To count till the clock strike nine."

" I'll have none of your gold and silver,
    Nor none of your white money;
But I'll have bonny Jeany Gordon,
    And she shall go now with me."

Then she came tripping down the stair,
    With the tear into her eye;
One babe was at her foot,
    Another upon her knee.

" You're welcome, bonny Jeany Gordon,
With my young family;
Mount and go to Northumberland,
There a countess thou shall be."

SONG VIII.

JOHNY FAA, THE GYPSIE LADDY.*

The gyp-sics came to our good lord's gate, And wow but they sang sweet-ly; They sang sae sweet,

* A person of this name (John Faw) is said to have been king of the gypsies in the time of James VI., who, about the year 1595, issued a proclamation, ordaining all sheriffs, &c., to assist him in seizing and securing fugitive gypsies, and to lend him their prisons, stocks, fetters, &c., for that purpose: charging his lieges not to molest the said Faw and his company in their lawful business within the realm, or in passing through, remaining in, or going forth of the same, under penalty: and all skippers, masters of ships, and mariners, to receive him and his company upon their expenses for furthering them to parts beyond sea.—See M'Laurin's *Remarkable Cases*, p. 774.

The Faws, Faas, or Falls, were noted thieves in the neighbourhood of Greenlaw, where some persons of that name are said to be still remaining.

In 1677 there happened a sharp conflict at Romanno in Tweeddale, between the Faws and the Shaws, two clans of gypsies, who, on their march from Haddington fair, to fight two other gangs, the

and sae ver-y com-pleat, That down came the fair la-dy. And she came trip-ping down the stair, And a' her maids be-fore her; As soon as they saw her well-far'd face, They coost the gla-mer o'er her.

> " Gar tak frae me this gay mantile,
> And bring to me a plaidie ;
> For if kith and kin and a' had sworn,
> I 'll follow the gypsie laddie.

Baillies and the Browns, had quarrelled about the division of the spoil. Several were killed and wounded on each side, and old Shaw and his three sons soon afterwards taken and hanged.—See Pennecuik's *Description of the Shire of Tweeddale*, 4to, 1715, p. 14.

No particular information has been obtained as to the hero of this ballad, but a different and more inaccurate copy may possibly furnish us with the rank and title of his mistress.

> There was seven gypsies in a gang,
> And they was brisk and bonny O,
> And they're to be hang'd all on a row
> For the Earl of Castle's * lady O.

Neighbouring tradition, it is said, strongly vouches for the truth of the story.

---

* Cassilis'.

" Yestreen I lay in a well-made bed,
   And my good lord beside me;
This night I 'll ly in a tenant's barn.
   Whatever shall betide me."

" Come to your bed," says Johny Faa,
   " Oh, come to your bed, my deary;
For I vow and swear by the hilt of my sword,
   That your lord shall nae mair come near ye."

" I 'll go to bed to my Johny Faa,
   And I 'll go to bed to my deary;
For I vow and swear by what past yestreen,
   That my lord shall nae mair come near me.

" I 'll mak a hap to my Johny Faa,
   And I 'll mak a hap to my deary;
And he 's get a' the coat gaes round,
   And my lord shall nae mair come near me."

And when our lord came home at e'en,
   And speir'd for his fair lady,
The tane she cry'd, and the other reply'd,
   " She 's away wi' the gypsie laddie."

" Gae saddle to me the black, black steed,
   Gae saddle and mak him ready;
Before that I either eat or sleep,
   I 'll gae seek my fair lady."

And we were fifteen well-made men,
    Although we were nae bonny;
And we were a' put down for ane,
    A fair young wanton lady.

SONG IX.

WHA WILL BAKE, ETC.

"WHA will bake my bridal bread,
    And brew my bridal ale?
And wha will welcome my brisk bride,
    That I bring o'er the dale?"

"I will bake your bridal bread,
    And brew your bridal ale;
And I will welcome your brisk bride,
    That you bring o'er the dale."

"But she that welcomes my brisk bride
    Maun gang like maiden fair,
She maun lace on her robe sae jimp,
    And braid her yellow hair."

"But how can I gang maiden-like,
    When maiden I am nane?
Have I not born seven sons to thee,
    And am with child agen?"

She 's taen her young son in her arms,
   Another in her hand,
And she 's up to the highest tower,
   To see him come to land.

" You 're welcome to your house, master,
   You 're welcome to your land,
You 're welcome with your fair lady,
   That you lead by the hand."

   .   .   .   .   .

And aye she served the lang tables,
   With white bread and with wine;
And aye she drank the wan water,
   To had her colour fine.

Now he 's ta'en down a silk napkin,
   Hung on a silver pin,
And aye he wipes the tear trickling
   Adown her cheek and chin.

SONG X.

YOUNG WATERS.*

A - bout Zule, quhen the wind blew cule, And the round tab-les be-gan, A'! there is cum to our king's court Mon-y a well-fa-vour'd man. The queen luikt owre the cas-tle wa', Be-held baith dale and down, And there she saw Zoung Wa-ters Cum rid-ing to the town.

His footmen they did rin before,
His horsemen rade behinde,
And mantel of the burning gowd
Did keep him frae the wind.

* Dr Percy tells us it had been suggested to him, that this ballad covertly alludes to the indiscreet partiality which Queen Anne of Denmark is said to have shown for the Earl of Murray, and which was supposed to have influenced the fate of that nobleman. In support of this conjecture he quotes the following passage (through the medium of the *Critical Review*) from Sir James Balfour's MS. annals in the Advocates' Library: "The seventh of Febry, this

Gowden graith'd his horse before,
And siller shod behind,
The horse Zoung Waters rade upon
Was fleeter than the wind.

Out then spack a wylie lord,
Unto the queen said he,
" O tell me quha's the fairest face
Rides in the company."

" I've sene lord, and I 've sene laird,
And knights of high degree,
Bot a fairer face than Zoung Waters
Mine eyne did never see."

Out then spack the jealous king,
(And an angry man was he)
" O ! if he had bin twice as fair,
Zou micht have excepted me."

zeire, 1592, the Earle of Murray was cruelly murthered by the Earle of Huntley, at his house in Dunibrissel in Fyffeshyre, and with him Dunbar, Sheriffe of Murray. It was given out and publickly talkt, that the Earle of Huntley was only the instrument of perpetrating this facte, to satisfie the king's jealousie of Murray, quhum the queene, more rashely than wisely, some few days before, had commendit in the king's hearing, with too many epithets of a proper and gallant man. The reasons of these surmises proceedit from a proclamatione of the king's, the 13 of Marche following, inhibitcine the zoung Earle of Murray to pursue the Earle of Huntley for his father's slaughter, in respect he being wardeit in the castell of Blacknesse for the same murther, was willing to abide a tryall, averring that he had done nothing but by the king's majestie's commissione ; and was neither airt nor part in the murther."

"Zou're neither laird nor lord," she says,
　"Bot the king that wears the crown;
There's not a knight in fair Scotland
　Bot to thee maun bow down."

For a' that she could do or say,
　Appeased he wad nae bee;
Bot for the words which she had said
　Zoung Waters he maun die.

They hae taen Zoung Waters, and
　Put fetters to his feet;
They hae taen Zoung Waters, and
　Thrown him in dungeon deep.

Aft I have ridden through Stirling town,
　In the wind bot and the weit;
Bot I neir rade through Stirling town
　Wi' fetters at my feet.

Aft I have ridden through Stirling town
　In the wind bot and the rain;
But I neir rade through Stirling town,
　Neir to return again.

They hae taen to the heiding-hill
　His zoung son in his craddle;
And they hae taen to the heiding-hill
　His horse bot and his saddle.

They hae taen to the heiding-hill
His lady fair to see;
And for the words the queen had spoke,
Zoung Waters he did die.

SONG XI.

THE CRUEL KNIGHT.

The knight stands in the sta-ble door, As he was for to ryde, When out their came his fair la-dy, De-sir-ing him to byde.

"How can I byde, how dare I byde,
How can I byde with thee?
Have I not kill'd thy ae brother?
Thou had'st nae mair but he."

"If you have kill'd my ae brother,
Alas! and woe is me!
But if I save your fair body,
The better you'll like me."

She's tane him to her secret bower,
　　Pinn'd with a siller pin ;
And she's up to her highest tower,
　　To watch that none come in.

She had na well gane up the stair,
　　And entered in her tower,
When four and twenty armed knights
　　Came riding to the door.

"Now, God you save, my fair lady,
　　I pray you tell to me,
Saw you not a wounded knight
　　Come riding by this way?"

"Yes ; bloody, bloody was his sword,
　　And bloody were his hands ;
But if the steed he rides be good,
　　He's past fair Scotland's strands.

"Light down, light down, then, gentlemen,
　　And take some bread and wine ;
The better you will him pursue,
　　When you shall lightly dine."

"We thank you for your bread, lady,
　　We thank you for your wine ;
I would gie thrice three thousand pounds
　　Your fair body was mine."

Then she's gane to her secret bower,
    Her husband dear to meet;
But out he drew his bloody sword,
    And wounded her sae deep.

"What aileth thee now, good my lord,
    What aileth thee at me?
Have you not got my father's gold,
    But and my mother's fee?"

"Now live, now live, my fair lady,
    O live but half an hour;
There's ne'er a leech in fair Scotland,
    But shall be at thy bower."

"How can I live, how shall I live,
    How can I live for thee?
See you not where my red heart's blood
    Runs trickling down my knee?"

SCOTISH SONGS.

SONG XII.

LORD THOMAS AND FAIR ANNET.*

Lord Tho - mas and fair An - net Sate a' day on a hill; When night was cum, and the sun was set, They had not talkt their fill.

Lord Thomas said a word in jest,
    Fair Annet took it ill :
" A' ! I will nevir wed a wife
    Against my ain friends' will."

" Gif ye wull nevir wed a wife,
    A wife wull neir wed yee."
Sae he is hame to tell his mither,
    And knelt upon his knee :

" O rede, O rede," mither, he says,
    " A gude rede gie to mee ;
O sall I tak the nut-browne bride,
    And let faire Annet bee ? "

---

* This ballad, it is observed by the editor of the " Reliques of Ancient English Poetry," seems to be composed (not without improvements) out of two ancient English ones printed in that collection,—viz., "Lord Thomas and Fair Ellinor," and "Fair Margaret and Sweet William."

"The nut-browne bride haes gowd and gear,
　Fair Annet she has gat nane;
And the little beauty fair Annet has,
　O it wull soon be gane!"

And he has till his brother gane:
　"Now, brother, rede ye mee;
A' sall I marrie the nut-browne bride,
　And let fair Annet bee?"

"The nut-browne bride has oxen, brother,
　The nut-browne bride has kye;
I wad hae ye marrie the nut-browne bride,
　And cast fair Annet bye."

"Her oxen may dye i' the house, Billie,
　And her kye into the byre;
And I sall hae nothing to my sell,
　Bot a fat fadge by the fyre."

And he has till his sister gane:
　"Now, sister, rede ye me;
O sall I marrie the nut-browne bride,
　And set fair Annet free?"

"Ise rede ye tak fair Annet, Thomas,
　And let the browne bride alane;
Lest ye sould sigh and say, Alace!
　What is this we brought hame?"

"No, I will tak my mither's counsel,
  And marrie me owt o' hand;
And I will tak the nut-browne bride;
  Fair Annet may leive the land."

Up then rose fair Annet's father,
  Twa hours or it wer day,
And he is gane into the bower
  Wherein fair Annet lay.

"Rise up, rise up, fair Annet," he says,
  "Put on your silken sheene;
Let us gae to St Marie's kirke,
  And see that rich weddeen."

"My maides, gae to my dressing-roome,
  And dress to me my hair,
Whair-eir yee laid a plait before,
  See yee lay ten times mair.

"My maides, gae to my dressing-room,
  And dress to me my smock;
The one half is o' the holland fine,
  The other o' needle-work."

The horse fair Annet rade upon,
  He amblit like the wind,
Wi' siller he was shod before,
  Wi' burning gowd behind.

SCOTISH SONGS.

Four-and-twanty siller bells
    Wer a' tyed till his mane,
And at ae tift o' the norland wind,
    They tinkled ane by ane.

Four-and-twanty gay gude knichts
    Rade by fair Annet's side,
And four-and-twanty fair ladies,
    As gin she had bin a bride.

And whan she cam to Marie's kirke,
    She sat on Marie's stein;
The cleading that fair Annet had on
    It skinkled in their een.

And whan she cam into the kirk,
    She shimmer'd like the sun;
The belt that was about her waist,
    Was a' wi' pearles bedone.

She sat her by the nut-browne bride,
    And her een they wer sae clear,
Lord Thomas he clean forgat the bride,
    When fair Annet she drew near.

He had a rose into his hand,
    And he gave it kisses three,
And, reaching it by the nut-browne bride,
    Laid it on fair Annet's knee.

Up than spak the nut-browne bride,
   She spak wi' meikle spite ;
"And whair gat ye that rose-water,
   That does mak yee sae white ?"

"Oh I did get that rose-water
   Whair ye wull neir get nane,
For I did get that very rose-water,
   Into my mither's wame."

The bride she drew a long bodkin,
   Frae out her gay head-gear,
And strake fair Annet unto the heart,
   That word she nevir spak mair.

Lord Thomas he saw fair Annet wex pale,
   And marvelit what mote bee ;
But whan he saw her dear heart's blude,
   A' wood-wroth wexed hee.

He drew his dagger, that was sae sharp,
   That was sae sharp and meet,
And drave it into the nut-browne bride,
   That fell deid at his feit.

"Now stay for me, dear Annet," he sed,
   "Now stay, my dear," he cry'd ;
Then strake the dagger untill his heart,
   And fell deid by her side.

Lord Thomas was buried without the kirk-wa',
  Fair Annet within the quiere;
And o' the tane thair grew a birk,
  The other a bonny briere.

And aye they grew, and aye they threw,
  As they wad faine be neare;
And by this ye may ken right weil,
  They were twa luvers deare.

SONG XIII.

WILLY AND ANNET.

Lived ance twa luv-ers in you dale, And they loved i-ther weel, Frae ev'n-ing late to morn-ing aire Of luv-ing luved their fill. Frae ev'n-ing late to morn-ing aire, Of luv-ing luved their fill.

2 L

"And we will sail the sea sae green,
    Unto some far countrie,
Or we'll sail to some bonnie isle,
    Stands lanely midst the sea."

But lang or ere the schip was built,
    Or deck'd, or rigged out,
Came sick a pain in Annet's back,
    That down she cou'd na lout.

"Now, Willie, gif ye luve me weel,
    As sae it seems to me,
Oh haste, haste, bring me to my bower,
    And my bower-maidens three."

He's taen her in his arms twa,
    And kiss'd her cheik and chin;
He's brocht her to her ain sweet bower,
    But nae bower-maid was in.

"Now, leave my bower, Willie," she said,
    "Now leave me to my lane;
Was nevir man in a lady's bower
    When she was travelling."

He's stepped three steps down the stair,
    Upon the marble stane,
Sae loud's he heard his young son's greet,
    But and his lady's mane!

"Now come, now come, Willie," she said,
  "Tak your young son frae me,
And hie him to your mother's bower,
  With speed and privacie."

He's taen his young son in his arms,
  He's kiss'd him cheik and chin,
He's hied him to his mother's bower,
  By th' ae light of the moon.

And with him came the bold barone,
  And he spake up wi' pride,
"Gar seek, gar seek the bower-maidens,
  Gar busk, gar busk the bryde."

"My maidens, easy with my back,
  And easy with my side;
Oh set my saddle saft, Willie,
  I am a tender bryde."

When she came to the burrow town,
  They gied her a broach and ring;
And when she came to * * * *
  They had a fair wedding.

Oh up then spake the Norland lord,
  And blinkit wi' his ee,
"I trow this lady's born a bairn;"
  Then leucht loud lauchters three.

And up then spake the brisk bridegroom,
    And he spake up wi' pryde;
"Gin I should pawn my wedding-gloves,
    I will dance wi' the bryde."

"Now had your tongue, my lord," she said,
    "Wi' dancing let me be;
I am sae thin in flesh and blude,
    Sma' dancing will serve me."

But she's taen Willie be the hand,
    The tear blinded her ee,
"But I wad dance wi' my true love—
    But bursts my heart in three."

She's taen her bracelet frae her arm,
    Her garter frae her knee,
"Gie that, gie that to my young son,
    He'll ne'er his mother see."

    .   .   .

"Gar deal, gar deal the bread, mother,
    Gar deal, gar deal the wyne;
This day hath seen my true luve's death,
    This nicht shall witness myne."

SONG XIV.

BONNY BARBARA ALLAN.

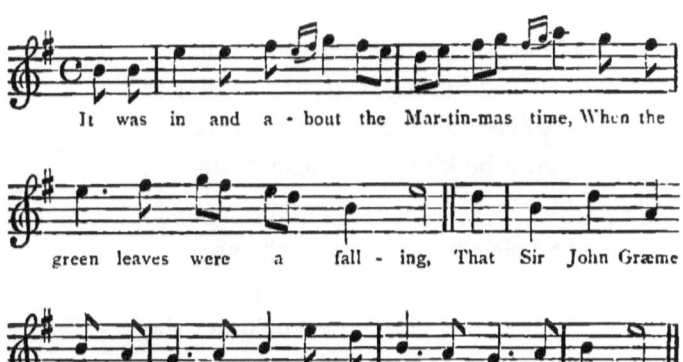

It was in and a-bout the Mar-tin-mas time, When the green leaves were a fall-ing, That Sir John Græme in the west coun-try Fell in love with Bar-bara Al-lan.

He sent his man down through the town,
    To the place where she was dwelling:
" Oh haste and come to my master dear,
    Gin ye be Barbara Allan."

Oh hooly, hooly rose she up,
    To the place where he was lying;
And when she drew the curtain by,
    " Young man, I think you're dying."

" Oh, its I'm sick, and very very sick,
    And 'tis a' for Barbara Allan."
" Oh, the better for me ye's never be,
    Though your heart's blood were a spilling."

"Oh dinna ye mind, young man," said she,
　"When ye was in the tavern a drinking,
That ye made the healths gae round and round,
　And slighted Barbara Allan?"

He turn'd his face unto the wall,
　And death was with him dealing:
"Adieu, adieu, my dear friends all,
　And be kind to Barbara Allan."

And slowly, slowly raise she up,
　And slowly, slowly left him;
And, sighing, said, she cou'd not stay,
　Since death of life had reft him.

She had not gane a mile but twa,
　When she heard the dead-bell ringing,
And every jow that the dead-bell geid,
　It cry'd, Woe to Barbara Allan.

"O mother, mother make my bed,
　O make it saft and narrow;
Since my love died for me to-day,
　I'll die for him to-morrow."

———◆———

SONG XV.

HERO AND LEANDER.

Le - an - der on the bay Of Hel - les - pont all na - ked stood, Im - pa - tient of de - lay, He leapt in - to the fa - tal flood: The rag - ing seas, Whom none can please,'Gainst him their ma - lice show; The hea - vens lower'd, The rain down pour'd, And loud the winds did blow.

Then casting round his eyes,
   Thus of his fate he did complain:
Ye cruel rocks and skies!
   Ye stormy winds, and angry main!
     What 'tis to miss
     The lover's bliss,
Alas! ye do not know;
     Make me your wreck
     As I come back,
But spare me as I go.

Lo! yonder stands the tower
   Where my beloved Hero lyes,
And this is the appointed hour
   Which sets to watch her longing eyes.
      To his fond suit
      The gods were mute;
The billows answer, No:
      Up to the skies
      The surges rise,
But sunk the youth as low.

Meanwhile the wishing maid,
   Divided 'twixt her care and love,
Now does his stay upbraid,
   Now dreads he should the passage prove:
      O fate! said she,
      Nor heaven, nor thee,
Our vows shall e'er divide;
      I'd leap this wall,
      Could I but fall
By my Leander's side.

At length the rising sun
   Did to her sight reveal, too late,
That Hero was undone;
   Not by Leander's fault, but fate.
      Said she, I'll show,
      Though we are two,
Our loves were ever one:
      This proof I'll give,
      I will not live,
Nor shall he die alone.

Down from the wall she leapt
    Into the raging seas to him,
Courting each wave she met
    To teach her weary'd arms to swim:
        The sea-gods wept,
        Nor longer kept
Her from her lover's side;
        When join'd at last,
        She grasp'd him fast,
Then sigh'd, embraced, and died.

SONG XVI.

SWEET WILLIAM'S GHOST.

There came a ghost to Mar-g'ret's door, With many a griev-ous groan; And aye he tirl-ed at the pin, But an-swer made she none.

"Is that my father Philip?
    Or is't my brother John?
Or is't my true love Willy,
    From Scotland new come home?"

"'Tis not thy father Philip,
    Nor yet thy brother John;
But 'tis thy true love Willy,
    From Scotland new come home.

O sweet Marg'ret! O dear Marg'ret!
    I pray thee speak to me;
Give me my faith and troth, Marg'ret,
    As I gave it to thee."

"Thy faith and troth thou's never get,
    Nor yet will I thee lend,
Till that thou come within my bower,
    And kiss my cheek and chin."

"If I should come within thy bower,
    I am no earthly man;
And should I kiss thy rosy lips,
    Thy days will not be lang.

O sweet Marg'ret! O dear Marg'ret!
    I pray thee speak to me;
Give me my faith and troth, Marg'ret,
    As I gave it to thee."

"Thy faith and troth thou 's never get,
    Nor yet will I thee lend,
Till you take me to yon kirk-yard,
    And wed me with a ring."

"My bones are buried in yon kirk-yard,
    Afar beyond the sea ;
And it is but my spirit, Marg'ret,
    That's now speaking to thee."

She stretch'd out her lily-white hand,
    And for to do her best,
"Hae, there's your faith and troth, Willy,
    God send your soul good rest."

Now she has kilted her robes of green
    A piece below her knee,
And a' the live-lang winter night
    The dead corp follow'd she.

"Is there any room at your head, Willy,
    Or any room at your feet ;
Or any room at your side, Willy,
    Wherein that I may creep ?"

"There's no room at my head, Marg'ret,
    There's no room at my feet ;
There's no room at my side, Marg'ret,
    My coffin's made so meet."

Then up and crew the red, red cock,
    And up then crew the gray :
"'Tis time, 'tis time, my dear Marg'ret,
    That you were going away."

540 SCOTISH SONGS.

No more the ghost to Marg'ret said,
  But with a grievous groan,
Evanish'd in a cloud of mist,
  And left her all alone.

" O stay, my only true love, stay,"
  The constant Marg'ret cry'd ;
Wan grew her cheeks, she closed her een,
  Stretch'd her soft limbs and dy'd.*

SONG XVII.

WILLIAM AND MARGARET.†

BY DAVID MALLET, ESQ.

'Twas at the si-lent, sol-emn hour, When night and morn-ing meet, In glid-ed Mar-g'ret's grim-ly ghost, and stood at Wil-liam's feet.

* The two last stanzas were probably added by Ramsay : they are evidently spurious.

† The following account of this beautiful ballad is given by the author in his works :—

" *N.B.*—In a comedy of FLETCHER, called *The Knight of the*

Her face was like an April-morn,
  Clad in a wintry cloud !
And clay-cold was her lily hand,
  That held her sable shroud.

So shall the fairest face appear,
  When youth and years are flown :
Such is the robe that kings must wear,
  When death has reft their crown.

Her bloom was like the springing flower,
  That sips the silver dew ;
The rose was budded in her cheek,
  Just opening to the view.

Burning Pestle, old MERRY-THOUGHT enters repeating the following verses :—

  "When it was grown to dark midnight,
    And all were fast asleep,
  In came Marg'ret's grimly ghost,
    And stood at William's feet."

"This was probably the beginning of some ballad, commonly known at the time when that author wrote ; and it is all of it, I believe, that is anywhere to be met with. These lines, naked of ornament and simple as they are, struck my fancy ; and, bringing fresh into my mind an unhappy adventure, much talked of formerly, gave birth to the foregoing poem, which was written many years ago."

The entire ballad, of which the above stanza had so fortunate an effect, may be found in Dr Percy's *Reliques*, vol. iii., and the *Select Collection of English Songs*, vol. ii. The "unhappy adventure" here alluded to was the real history of a young lady, whose hand having been scornfully rejected by her insolent seducer, "the news was brought her when in a weak condition, and cast her into a fever. And in a few days after, I," says Mr Mallet, "saw her and her child laid in one grave together." See the *Plain Dealer*, (a periodical paper, published by Mr Aaron Hill and Mr Bond, in 1724, and afterward reprinted in two vols. 8vo,) Nos. 36 and 46.

But Love had, like the canker worm,
   Consumed her early prime;
The rose grew pale, and left her cheek;
   She dy'd before her time.

"Awake!" she cry'd, "thy true love calls,
   Come from her midnight-grave;
Now let thy pity hear the maid,
   Thy love refused to save.

"This is the dumb and dreary hour,
   When injured ghosts complain;
When yawning graves give up their dead,
   To haunt the faithless swain.

"Bethink thee, William, of thy fault,
   Thy pledge and broken oath:
And give me back my maiden-vow,
   And give me back my troth.

"Why did you promise love to me,
   And not that promise keep?
Why did you swear my eyes were bright,
   Yet leave those eyes to weep?

"How could you say my face was fair,
   And yet that face forsake?
How could you win my virgin heart,
   Yet leave that heart to break?

" Why did you say my lip was sweet,
    And made the scarlet pale?
Why did I, young witless maid!
    Believe the flattering tale?

" That face, alas! no more is fair,
    Those lips no longer red;
Dark are my eyes now closed in death,
    And every charm is fled.

" The hungry worm my sister is,
    This winding-sheet I wear;
And cold and weary lasts our night,
    Till that last morn appear.

" But hark! the cock has warn'd me hence,
    A long and late adieu!
Come, see, false man, how low she lies,
    Who dy'd for love of you."

The lark sang loud, the morning smiled,
    With beams of rosy red;
Pale William quaked in every limb,
    And raving left his bed.

He hy'd him to the fatal place,
    Where Margaret's body lay;
And stretch'd him on the grass-green turf,
    That wrapp'd her breathless clay.

And thrice he call'd on Margaret's name,
And thrice he wept full sore;
Then laid his cheek to her cold grave,
And word spoke never more.

INDEX OF FIRST LINES.

	PAGE
About Zule quhen the wind blew cule,	518
A cock laird, fu' cadgie,	247
Adieu, ye streams that smoothly glide,	224
A freen' o' mine cam' here yestreen,	182
Ah! gaze not on those eyes,	165
Ah! the (poor) shepherd's mournful fate,	168
A hoary swain, inured to care,	434
Alas! my son, you little know,	193
Alas! when charming Sylvia's gone,	154
A lass that was laden wi' care,	206
And ye sall walk in silk attire,	210
An thou were my ain thing,	123
As I came in by Auchendown,	382
As I cam' in by Teviot side,	176
As I was a walking ae May morning,	187
As I was walking all alone,	478
As Sylvia in a forest lay,	221
As walking forth, to view the plain,	127
Awake, my love; with genial ray,	140
Awa', Whigs, awa',	437
Aye wakin', oh!	150
A youth adorned with every art,	222
Baloo, my boy, lie still and sleep,	237
Be mirry, bretherene, ane and all,	313
Beneath a green shade, a lovely young swain,	166
Blythe, blythe, and merry was she,	327
Busk ye, busk ye, my bonnie, bonnie bride,	227
But are ye sure the news is true,	180
By Pinkie House oft let me walk,	138
By yon castle wa', at the close of the day,	423
Care, away go thou from me,	372

INDEX OF FIRST LINES.

	PAGE
Carl, an the king come,	388
Clavers and his Highlandmen,	385
Coming through the broom at e'en,	178
Cope sent a challenge to Dunbar,	424
Dear batchelor, I've read your billet,	309
Did ever swain a nymph adore,	169
Doun in yon meadow a couple did tarry,	294
Fareweel to a' our Scotish fame,	394
Farewell, thou fair day,	453
Farewell to Lochaber,	196
Farewell, ye dungeons dark and strong,	457
For ever, Fortune, wilt thou prove,	143
For the lack of gold she's left me, O!	192
From anxious zeal, and factious strife,	145
Fy, let us all to the briddel,	277
Get up, gudewife, don on your claise,	289
Gilderoy was a bonny, bonny boy,	368
Gil Morrice was an erle's son,	495
Good morrow, fair mistress,	195
Go plaintive sounds, and to the fair,	146
Hearken, and I will tell you how,	268
Hear me, ye nymphs, and every swain,	190
Here awa', there awa', here awa', Willie,	179
Here's a health to all brave English lads,	427
How blythe ilk morn was I to see,	202
How happy is the rural clown,	184
I am a batchelor winsome,	307
I chanced to meet an airy blade,	253
I hae laid a herring in saut,	258
I lo'e na a laddie but ane,	260
I mak it kend, he that will spend,	321
In April, when primroses paint the sweet plain,	125
In summer I mawed my meadow.	148
In the land of Fife, there lived a wicked wife,	302
In winter when the rain rain'd cauld,	286
It fell about the Martinmas time,	292
It fell about the Martinmas,	362
It's I hae seven braw new gowns,	305
It's no very lang sin' syne,	188
It was in and about the Martinmas time,	533
It was in old times, when trees composed rhymes,	392
I've heard them liltin', at the ewes milkin',	347

INDEX OF FIRST LINES.

	PAGE
I've seen the smiling of Fortune beguiling,	449
I've spent my time in rioting,	454
I wish I were where Helen lies,	225
Jocky said to Jenny,	259
Late in an evening forth I went,	283
Leander on the bay,	535
Let mournful Britons now deplore,	433
Lithe and listen, gentlemen,	469
Little wat ye wha's coming,	395
Lived ance twa luvers in yon dale,	529
Look where my dear Hamilla smiles,	122
Lord Thomas and fair Annet sate a' day on a hill,	524
Love never more shall give me pain,	215
March, march! Why the deil d'ye na march?	380
Murn ye heighlands, and murn ye leighlands,	358
My daddie is a canker'd carle,	149
My dear and only love I pray,	160
My father has forty gude shillings,	303
My Harry was a gallant gay,	448
My love has built a bonnie ship,	216
My love was born in Aberdeen,	430
My mither's aye glowrin' o'er me,	137
My Peggy is a young thing,	119
My sheep I neglected,	198
Nancy's to the greenwood gane,	255
Now wat ye wha I met yestreen,	135
Oh! come awa', come awa', come awa' wi' me, Jeany,	157
O! haud awa', bide awa', haud awa' frae me, Donald,	158
Oh! how can I be blythe and glad,	211
Oh! how shall I venture, or dare to reveal,	444
Oh! I hae lost my silken snood,	186
O! Kenmure's on and awa', Willie,	397
O! listen, gude peopell, to my tale,	503
Oh! send my Lewis Gordon hame,	445
Oh! waly, waly up the bank,	235
O! were I able to rehearse,	342
O! Willie brew'd a peck o' maut,	320
O! will ye hae ta tartan plaid,	261
O! wouldst thou know her sacred charms,	117
Of all the things beneath the sun,	311
On Ettrick's banks on a summer night,	133
Our gudeman cam' hame at e'en,	296

	PAGE
Pray, came ye here the fight to shun,	409
Quhy dois your brand sae drop wi' bluid,	480
Robeyn's Jok come to wow our Jynny,	264
Stately stept he east the wa',	482
Sum speiks of lords, sum speiks of lairds,	351
Sweet Annie frae the sea beach came,	208
Sweet sir, for your courtesie,	249
Tarry woo', tarry woo', tarry woo' is ill to spin,	340
The chevalier, being void of fear,	417
The Duke of Gordon has three daughters,	507
The gypsies came to our good lord's gate,	513
The king sits in Dunfermling toune,	349
The lass o' Patie's mill,	129
The last time I came o'er the moor,	199
The meal was dear short syne,	271
The pawky auld carle came o'er the lea,	241
The smiling morn, the breathing spring,	141
The smiling plains, profusely gay,	142
The spring-time returns, and clothes the green,	174
The sun sets in night,	467
There came a ghost to Marg'ret's door,	537
There's auld Rob Morris,	251
There's some say that we wan,	399
There was a jolly beggar,	245
There was an auld wife had a wee pickle tow,	334
There was ance a may, and she lo'ed na men,	212
There was a wife wonn'd in a glen,	331
Thickest night, surround my dwelling,	446
Thy braes were bonnie, Yarrow stream,	233
Thy fatal shafts unerring move,	173
Though Geordie reigns in Jamie's stead,	441
To daunton me, to daunton me,	450
'Twas at the silent solemn hour,	540
Wha will bake my bridal bread,	516
Wha wadna be in love,	324
What beauties does Flora disclose,	120
What can a young lassie,	301
When Britain first, at heaven's command,	465
When first my dear laddie ga'ed to the green hill,	132
When Frennet castle's ivied walls,	374
When Guilford good our pilot stood,	462
When I hae a saxpence under my thoom,	318

INDEX OF FIRST LINES.

	PAGE
When I think on this warld's pelf,	317
When I was in my se'nteen year,	281
When Phœbus bright the azure skies,	458
When Sappho struck the quiv'ring wire,	131
When summer comes, the swains on Tweed,	205
When the sheep are in the fauld,	218
When we went to the field of war,	414
Where art thou, Hope,	162
Why hangs that cloud upon thy brow,	155
Willie was a wanton wag,	327
Willy's rare, and Willy's fair,	223
Will ye go to Flanders, my Mally, O?	151
Will ye go to the ewe-bughts, Marion?	152
Woo'd and married and a',	275
Ye highlands, and ye lawlands,	372
Ye Jacobites by name, give an ear,	452
Ye shepherds and nymphs that adorn,	172
Ye warlike men, with tongue and pen,	431
Ye woods, ye mountains unknown,	201
You're welcome, Charley Stuart,	438

INDEX OF SONGS AND TUNES.

	PAGE
Adam of Gordon,	362
Adieu, ye streams,	224
A hoary swain, inured to care,	434
Alas! that I cam' o'er the moor,	199
Alas! when charming Silvia's gone,	154
Alloa house,	174
An address to his mistress,	142
Andro and his cutty gun,	327
An the kirk wad let me be,	305
An thou were my ain thing,	123
Auld Robin Gray,	218
Auld Rob Morris,	251
A Scotch brawle,	289
Awa', Whigs, awa',	437
Aye wakin', oh!	150
A youth adorn'd with every art,	222
Ballat of gude-fallowis,	321
Billet by Jeany Gradden,	309
Blink over the burn, sweet Betty,	148
Bonny Barbara Allan,	533
Cameron's march,	409
Care, away go thou from me,	322
Carl, an the king come,	388
harming Highlandman,	445
Cope, are you waking yet?	424
Cumbernauld house,	145
Drucken wife o' Galloway,	294
Drummossie day,	433
Edinburgh Katie's answer,	137

INDEX OF SONGS AND TUNES. 551

	PAGE
Edward, Edward,	480
Ettrick banks,	133
Ewe-bughts, Marion,	152
Fair Annie, (wha will bake my bridal bread,)	516
Flodden field,	347
For a' that,	441
For the lack of gold she 's left me, O!	192
For the love of Jean,	259
Frennet hall,	374
Fy to the hills in the morning,	424
Galashiels,	168
Gala water,	178
General Lesly's march,	380
Get up and bar the door,	292
Gilderoy,	368
Gillicrankie,	385
Gil Morrice,	495
Good morrow, fair mistress,	195
Go plaintive sounds,	146
Hallowe'en,	155
Happy Dick Dawson,	260
Hardyknute,	482
Haud awa' frae me, Donald,	157, 261
Helen of Kirkconnell,	225
Hero and Leander,	535
Highlander's lament,	448
I 'll cheer up my heart,	187
I 'll never love thee more,	160
In honour of the Mayor of Carlisle,	431
Johnie Armstrong,	351
Johnie Coup,	426
Johnie Faa, the gypsie laddy,	513
Johnnie's grey breeks,	281
Katharine Ogie,	127
Lady Ann Bothwell's lament,	237
Lass gin ye lo'e me tell me now,	258
Leader haughs and Yarrow,	458
Lochaber no more,	196
Logan water,	143
Lord Thomas and fair Annet,	524

	PAGE
Low doun in the broom,	149
Macpherson's farewell,	457
Macpherson's lament,	454
Maggie Lauder,	324
Maggie's tocher,	271
Muirland Willie,	268
My apron, dearie,	198
My auld man,	302
My dearie, an thou dee,	215
My father has forty gude shillings,	303
My heart's my ain,	188
My jo Janet,	249
My wife's ta'en the gee,	182
Nae dominies for me, laddie,	253
O! Kenmure's on and awa', Willie,	397
Oh! how shall I venture, or dare to reveal,	444
Of all the things beneath the sun,	311
Of evil wyffis,	313
On Celia playing on the harpsichord,	131
Oran-an-aoig, or the song of death,	453
Our gudeman cam hame at e'en,	296
Pinkie house, or Rothe's lament,	138
Rare Willy drown'd in Yarrow,	223
Rothe's lament, or Pinkie house,	138
Rule Britannia,	465
Sae merry as we hae been,	206
Scornfu' Nancy,	255
Sheriffmuir,	399
Sir Patrick Spence,	349
Slighted love sair to bide,	162
Slighted Nancy,	305
Strathallan's lament,	446
Such a parcel of rogues in a nation,	394
Sweet Annie,	208
Sweet William's ghost,	537
Tak your auld cloak about ye,	286
Tarry woo',	340
The auld gudeman,	283
The auld wife ayont the fire,	331
The bagrie o't,	317

INDEX OF SONGS AND TUNES.   553

	PAGE
The banks of the Forth,	140
The battle of Corichie,	358
The birks of Invermay or Endermay,	141
The blathrie o't,	317
The blythsome bridal,	277
The bonny Earl of Murray,	372
The bonnie lad that's far awa',	211
The bonnie lass of Branksome,	176
The braes o' Ballendine,	166
The braes of Yarrow,	227, 233
The bridegroom grat,	218
The broom of Cowdenknowes,	202
The bush aboon Traquair,	190
The Campbells are coming,	427
The Chevalier's muster roll,	395
The clans,	427
The cock laird,	247
The death song of the Cherokee Indian,	467
The Duke of Gordon's daughter,	507
The ewie wi' the crooked horn,	342
The flowers of the forest,	347
The gaberlunzie man,	241
The gypsie laddie,	513
The happy clown,	184
The happy lover's reflections,	199
The haws of Cromdale,	382
The heir of Linne,	469
The jolly beggar,	245
The lass o' Patie's mill,	129
The lowlands of Holland,	216
The mariner's wife,	180
The rock and the wee pickle tow,	334
The siller crown,	210
The thistle and rose,	392
The vain advice,	165
The waukin' o' the fauld,	119
The wee wee man,	478
The white cockade,	430
The wowing of Jok and Jynny,	264
The yellow-haired laddie,	125
The young laird and Edinburgh Katie,	135
The young laird of Ochiltree,	503
There'll never be peace till Jamie comes hame,	423
Thy fatal shafts unerring move,	173
To a lady,	155
To daunton me,	450
To Mrs A. H.,	122

	PAGE
Toddlin' butt, and toddlin' ben,	318
Tranent muir,	417
Tweedside,	120
Twine weel the plaiden,	186
Ungrateful Nanny,	169
Up and war them a', Willie,	414
Waly, waly, gin love be bonnie,	235
Wandering Willie,	179
Wayward wife,	193
Welcome, Charley Stuart,	438
We'll kick the world before us,	188
Werena my heart licht I wad dee,	212
What ails the lasses at me,	307
What can a young lassie,	301
When Guildford good our pilot stood,	462
When summer comes,	205
William and Margaret,	540
Willie brew'd a peck o' maut,	320
Willie was a wanton wag,	327
Will ye go to Flanders, my Mally, O?	151
Willy and Annet,	529
Winter was cauld, (note,)	125
Woo'd and married and a',	275
Ye Jacobites by name,	452
Ye shepherds and ye nymphs,	172
Ye woods and mountains unknown,	201
Young Waters,	518

AUTHORS' NAMES.

Adams, Jean, 180.
Austin, Dr, 192.
Baillie, Lady Grissel, 212.
Barclay, Rev. John, 409.
Binning, Charles Lord, 169.
Blacklock, Thomas, D.D., 166.
Blamire, Susanna, 210.
Blyth, Johne, (nom de plume,) 321.
Burne, Nicol, 458.
Burns, Robert, 211, 301, 320, 394, 397, 423, 446, 448, 452, 453, 457.
Carnegie, James, 149.
Clunie, Rev. John, 260.
Cockburn, Mrs, 165, 449.
Crawford, Robert, 120, 122, 190, 205, 215.
Elliott, Sir Gilbert, 198.
Elliot, Jane, of Minto, 347.
Falconer, William, 142.
Flemyng, ——, 313.
Forbes, John, of Mary-culter, 358.
Geddes, Dr Alex., 445.
Graham, James, Marquis of Montrose, 160.
Graham, Janet, 193.
Halket, Sir Alex., 368.

Hamilton, William, of Bangour, 117, 146, 155, 168, 172, 227.
Hoadley, Dr John, 208.
Home, Miss, 224.
Hunter, Mrs, 467.
James V. of Scotland, 241, 245.
Lindsay, Lady Ann, 218.
Logan, Rev. John, 233.
MacLennan, Rev. Murdoch, 399.
Mallet, David, 141, 201, 222, 540.
Mitchell, Joseph, 138, 221.
Ramsay, Allan, 119, 125, 129, 132, 135, 137, 176, 196, 199.
Robertson, Alex., of Struan, 434.
Ross, Alex., Lochlee, 307, 309, 333.
Semple, Francis, of Beltrees, 277, 324.
Skinner, Rev. John, 342.
Skirving, Adam, 417, 426.
Smollett, Tobias, M.D., 131, 173.
Thomson, James, 143, 465.
Tytler, James, 258.
Walkinshaw, William, of Walkinshaw, 327.
Wardlaw, Lady, 482.
Watt, ——, 392.
Webster, Rev. Alex., 174.

GLOSSARY.

A—at, on; "a deid of night," *at dead of night;* "a fit," *on foot.*
A'—all.
Abee—alone; "let that abee," *let that alone.*
Abein—above.
Abeit—albeit, although.
Aboon—above.
Ae—one, only, sole, each, every; "thy ae brither," *thy only brother;* "at ae tift," *at each tift.*
Aff—off.
Afore—before.
Aik—oak.
Aiken—oaken.
Ain—own.
Air—early.
Aiten—oaten.
Aits—oats.
Alane—alone.
Alland—"*up alland*"—at once, without delay.
Anshach—misfortune.
An'—and.
An—if.
An, ane—one.
Ance—once.
Aneath—beneath.
Anes—once.
Aneist—next.
Anither—another.
Anter—(adventure,) chance, happen.
Arms—"in arms," *arm-in-arm;* in *each other's arms.*

Ase—ashes.
Asteer—astir; in a clatter or ferment.
Astonyed—stunned.
Atour, attowre—over, across, quite over.
Aucht—possession.
Aught—eight.
Auld—old.
Ava, avae—of all, at all.
Avow—vow.
Awa'—away.
Awee—a little.
Awow—an exclamation, denoting admiration or surprise.
Awsome—awful, frightful, terrible.
Ay—yes.
Aye—still, even, always, to this time.
Ayont—beyond.

Bade awa'—stayed away.
Bagrie—trash, trumpery.
Bailie—magistrate of a Scotish burgh; synonymous with *Alderman.*
Bairded—bearded.
Bairn—child.
Baith—both.
Baloo—hush.
Bandsters—men who bind up the sheaves after the reapers.
Bang, "bade the bang"—*stood out the fight.*
Bann'd—cursed.
Bannocks—thick cakes unleavened.
Baps—rolls of bread.

GLOSSARY. 557

Bardies—bardlings, diminutive of bards.
Barket, barkit—tanned, barked.
Basined, bawsand—white-faced like a badger. *Bawsin* or *bawson*, old English for a badger.
Bauld—bold.
Bawbee, baubie or baubee—a Scotish coin ; an *English halfpenny* is often so called in Scotland.
Bawty—a dog's name.
Be—by.
Bear, beer, or beir—barley.
Beats—baits.
Becked or becket—curtseyed.
Bedone—set.
Bee—*see* Abee.
Bees—wild bees, capricious humours, extravagant fancies.
Beforn—before.
Beit—mend, increase, raise.
Ben—in, within, the inner part of a house ; *see* Butt.
Bend—drink, to drink hard.
Benew—beneath, below.
Benison—blessing.
Benorth—to the northward of.
Bent—the open country; a coarse kind of grass, *Agrostis* of different sorts.
Berne—bairn, child.
Beuk—book.
Bewest—to the westward of.
Bicker—a wooden vessel with handles, used for drinking ale.
Bide—abide, stay.
Bield, bielding, or beild—shelter.
Big—to build.
Big on—make on, fall upon, attack.
Biggit—built.
Bigonet—a linen cap or coif.
Billy—brother.
Binged—curtseyed.
Birk—birch tree.
Birl, birle—to drink in society; to contribute one's share of a tavern-bill.
Birns—stalks of burnt heath or heather.
Bladderskate—a good-for-nothing fellow; an indiscreet, nonsensical talker.

Blasnit—bald; deprived of hair.
Blate—bashful.
Blathrie—foolish talking.
Blaw—blow.
Bledder—bladder.
Bleid—blood, bled.
Bleize—blaze.
Blenched, blencht—white, pale.
Blin—to stay, cease.
Blin'—blind.
Blink—glance, spark, sparkle, twinkle.
Blinkan', blinkin'—glancing, sparkling, twinkling, shining.
Blinkit, blinket — glanced, looked kindly.
Blurt, blirt—a violent burst of tears.
Boaked—retched.
Bobbing—dancing.
Bobbit—danced.
Bodies—folks, people, persons.
Bodin—provided, furnished.
Bogle—the game *hide and seek*.
Bonnilie, bonnily—prettily.
Bonnie, bonny, bonie, bony—pretty, handsome, beauteous, goodlike.
Boot—must, behoved to.
Borrowstoun merchant — merchant who resides in an incorporated town, in contradistinction to a pedlar, or travelling merchant.
Bot, but—without.
Bot and—besides, and also.
Bought—*see* Bught.
Bougills—bugles.
Boun, boune, or bowne—ready or prepared to go.
Bower—arbour, chamber, woman's apartment, boudoir.
Bow'r-maid, bow'r-woman — lady's-maid, chamber-maid.
Braw, bra'—brave, finely-apparelled, grand-like ; "a braw lad," *a handsome man.*
Bracken—*see* Breckan.
Brae—the side of a hill; a hill of no great height.
Brag—boast, crow over.
Braid—broad.

Brankit—dressed finely.
Brast—burst; swollen almost to bursting.
Brawny—stout, lusty.
Break—to become bankrupt.
Breeks, breiks—breeches.
Brechame—horse-collar.
Breckan—fern; *Pteris aquilina.*
Bree—broth; water in which anything is boiled.
Brenning—burning.
Brent—burnt.
Brent—smooth, not wrinkled.
Breere, briere—briar.
Briddel—bridal, wedding.
Brig, brigue—bridge.
Broach—brooch.
Brochis—hames or haims for a horse-collar.
Brok—broken and left over victuals.
Broo—*see* Bree.
Broom—*Cytisus Scoparius.*
Brose—oatmeal or peasemeal moistened with hot water, and seasoned with salt.
Bruik—enjoy, possess.
Brydell renze—bridle reins.
Buckies—large sea snails; spiral shells.
Buckskins—Virginians.
Buft—cuffed, thrashed.
Bught—a little fold for inclosing ewes at milking-time.
Bughtin'—inclosing sheep in a fold.
Bun—backside.
Bun, bunn—sweet cake or loaf, of the kind used at the New Year.
Burn, burnie, or burny—brook, rill, rivulet; "Lawrie's Burn," *River St Lawrence.*
Burneist—burnished, washed, rubbed.
Burrow's toun—burgh, corporate town.
Busk—deck, dress, prepare; "busk and boon," *make ready* or *prepare to go.*
Busket—dressed.
Buss—bush.
Butt, but—the kitchen; inferior or outer part of a house; *see* Ben.
But and—*see* Bot and.

Butter box—Dutchman.
Byde—wait, endure.
Byre—cowhouse.

Ca'—call, drive.
Ca'd—called; "ca'd the bicker aft about," *put the bicker frequently round.*
Caddels—cawdles, hot pot made of ale, sugar, and eggs.
Cadgie, caigie—brisk, hearty, cheerful, wanton.
Cadgily—cheerfully.
Caller, callour—cool, fresh, untainted.
Camstairie—riotous, froward, perverse
Can—'gan, began to.
Can—skill, knowledge.
Canker'd—ill-tempered, peevish.
Canna—cannot.
Canny—cautious, prudent, knowing, neat.
Cantraps, cantrips — charms, spells, tricks.
Canty—cheerful, merry.
Capper-nos'd—Bardolph-nosed.
Caps—wooden bowls for containing food, whether solid or fluid.
Carl, carle, carlie—old man, churl.
Carling, carlin—old woman or wife.
Carlings—pease birsled or broiled.
Cartes—cards.
Castocks, custocs—cores or piths of cabbage or colewort stalks.
Catyvis—caitiffs, niggards.
Cauk—chalk.
Cauld—cold.
Cauler, cauller—*see* Caller.
Cess—city tax; composition paid by the inhabitants of Scotland to freebooters for sparing their cattle, better known as *blackmail.*
Chap—person.
Chap—knock.
Chapped stocks—boiled cabbage beat up with butter.
Chappin—chopine, a fluid measure equal to an English quart.
Chast—chastity.

GLOSSARY.

Cheip—squeak, chirp, make the least noise.
Cheis—choose.
Chield—youth, young fellow.
Christendie—Christendom.
Cla'—*see* Claw.
Clag—fault, failing, incumbrance, clot.
Clag—to cover with mud or anything adhesive.
Claise—clothes.
Claithing, claithin'—clothing.
Clapping—patting, stroking kindly.
Claw—scratch the face of an enemy.
Claymore—broadsword.
Clead—clothe.
Clean—quite.
Cled—clad, clothed.
Cleiro—din ; shrill, loud noise.
Cliding—clothing.
Clinked—joined, clinched.
Cliver—clever, active.
Clocken-hen—hatching-hen.
Clok—beetle.
Clout—a stroke ; also to mend.
Clouted—mended with a patch.
Cock—to strut.
Cock-laird—petty laird, who himself cultivates all his estate.
Cocks—head-dresses.
Cocky—vain ; assuming an air of importance.
Coft—bought.
Cog—a pail, or hollow wooden vessel, differing from a bicker, which has handles.
Coggie—a small wooden bowl.
Cogues, coig—*see* Cog.
Collie, colly—the shepherd's dog.
Conjunct-fee—right of property granted in common to husband and wife.
Coost—cast.
Coots—literally bare ankles, but may also mean half-gaiters or spatterdashes.
Crack—chat.
Crack—" in a crack," *in an instant.*
Cragy, craigie—neck.
Craig, crag—rock.

Cramasie—crimson.
Cranshaks—bandy-legged persons.
Crap—crept.
Creill, creel—an ozier basket, or hamper, made to be carried on the back.
Crook—bend; "crook my knee," *pretend to be lame.*
Cross—Sci. of Edinburgh.
Crouse—brisk, smart, stout, lively.
Crowdie—oatmeal moistened with cold water.
Crowdy-mowdy—milk and meal boiled together.
Cud—could.
Cuddle—embrace, fondle.
Cummers—gossips, companions.
Corroch, currach (Gaelic)—a coracle, or small Highland fishing-boat; also a sledge.
Curches, courches—square pieces of linen, used in former times by women instead of caps or mutches.
Curtsey—*see* Curches.
Cutty—short ; "cutty gun," supposed to mean *a short tobacco pipe.*

Da', daw—a sluggard, lazy, tawdry hussy.
Daffin'—foolish diversion ; pastime, gaiety.
Daft—giddy, thoughtless, unwise.
Dandering—sauntering, going about idly.
Dang—put down, overcome, beaten, struck.
Darrd—glanced off harmless.
Dart—hit.
Dather—daughter.
Daunton, danton—intimidate, daunt.
Daw—*see* Da'.
Dawtie, dawty—darling, favourite.
Dead-bell—death-bell, passing-bell.
Deads—death.
Deal—distribute.
Dearie—little dear; a term of affection.
Dee—die.
Deid—dead, death.
De'il—devil.

Deme—dame, mother.
Deimt—deemed.
Descriving—describing.
Dighted, dichted—wiped, cleaned.
Dice—checker work; "set with mony a dice," *set with figures of dice.*
Dikes—ditches, walls.
Dilp—a trollop, slattern.
Dilse, dulse—edible sea-weed; *Rhodomenia palmata.*
Din—noise.
Ding—to beat, strike, overcome.
Dinna—do not.
Dinsom—noisy.
Disna—does not.
Dochter—daughter.
Docken—dock, *Rumex* of different kinds.
Dominies—parsons, ministers, pedagogues.
Don on—do on, put on.
Dool! an exclamation of sorrow, pain, grief, mourning, or the like.
Door—a sword (from Icelandic, *daur.*)
Dosend—benumbed, lifeless, cold, impotent.
Dought—could, was able, possessed strength.
Dour, doure—stout, obstinate, sullen.
Dow, doo—dove.
Dow—can, is able to, dare.
Dowie—sad, doleful, melancholy.
Downa—dare not, cannot, unable to do.
Doylt—stupid, confused.
Dozin—*see* Dosend.
Dragen—confections (from Droggis.)
Drammock—meal and water mixed raw.
Drappie—a little drop.
Dree, drie—suffer, endure; "as fast as she could drie," *as fast as she was able.*
Drieps—drops.
Dribbles—drops; "nor dribbles of drink rins through the draff," *i.e., no brewing of ale goes in, no drops of drink run through the malt, or grains.*

Drie—*see* Dree.
Dring—miser, covetous person, slow, dilatory.
Drouth—thirst, drought.
Drumbly, drumly—muddy, disturbed, dark, troubled.
Dub—a little pool, a puddle.
Dublaris—pewter dishes of a large size.
Duddies—rags, tatters.
Duddy—ragged, tattered.
Dud sark—bit shift; rag of a shirt.
Dule—dole, sorrow, grief, pain.
Duleful—doleful, sorrowful, painful.
Dulse—*see* Dilse.
Dung—put down, conquered.
Durk, dirk—Highland dagger.
Dwam, dwalm, dwaum—fainting-fit, swoon; to fade; decline in health.
Dyne—dinner, (rhythmi gratiâ). So, however, in another Scotish ballad, never printed;—
" The king bot and his nobles a'
Sat drinking at the wine;
He would ha' nane but his ae daughter
To wait on them *at dyne."*
—*Brown Robin.*

Eard—earth.
Earn—coagulate, curdle.
Easements—tenements, rooms.
E'e, ee—eye.
Eelist—deformity; what offends the eye.
Een—eyes.
E'en—even, evening; "at e'en,"*in the evening.*
E'ens—even as.
Eerie, eery, iry — timorous, sad, dreary.
Eild—age; "to eild," *to age.*
Eir—ever.
Elwand—a stick to measure an ell=37 inches.
Ery—*see* Eerie.
Eschew—avoid.
Ettled—attempted, aimed.

Ewebughts—folds for sheep.
Ewie—diminutive of ewe.

Fa'—fall.
Fadge—a thick loaf of bread; figuratively any coarse heap of stuff.
Fae, fay—faith.
Fain—glad'; "fidgin' fain," *itching with joy.*
Fairly, ferlie—a wonder; a strange event.
Fairntickl'd, fernitickled—freckled.
Fand—found.
Fan—when.
Fardles, farles—the fourth part of a cake, either of oatmeal or flour; sometimes the third, depending on the mode of dividing, before baking it.
Fare—go.
Fash—to trouble, to vex; "ne'er fash," *never vex yourself:* "fash nae mair wi' me," *trouble yourself no more about me.*
Fash'd na—troubled not.
Fat—what.
Faucht—fought.
Fauld—sheep fold.
Fauld—"mony fauld," *many fold, many times.*
Faun, fawn—fallen.
Fead—feud, hatred, quarrel.
Fause—false.
Fecht, fechtin'—fight, fighting.
Feck—part, quantity; "money feck," *of great account:* "maist feck," *the greatest part.*
Fecket—an under shirt, or under waistcoat.
Feingit—feigned.
Feind—devil.
Fere—a companion; "in fere," *together.*
Feris—companions.
Ferlit—wondered.
Ferss—fierce.
Fey—predestined; on the verge of death; under a fatality.

Fidder, fother—128 lbs; a cart load of anything, such as *hay* or *peats.*
Fidging—restless; *see* Fain.
Fit—foot; "a fit," *on foot.*
Flaik, flake—a hurdle.
Flaes—fleas.
Flees—flies.
Fleis—flees.
Fleeching—coaxing, flattering.
Fleg—fright, a panic.
Flet—scolded, flyted.
Flie—flea.
Flinders—splinters, pieces.
Flings—kicks.
Flouks, fleuks—flounders, flat-fish.
Flowan—flowing.
Flyte, flytin'—chide, scold, scolding.
Fodgel—fat, squat, plump.
Fog—the generic name for moss; after-grass.
Forby—besides.
Fore—"to the fore;" *remaining; in existence.*
Forfairn—forlorn, destitute.
Foregathered, forgatherit—encountered, met.
Forpit, forpet—fourth part of a peck.
Forsta' me—understand me.
Fou—drunk, full.
Fouk—folks, people.
Fourugh, fooroch—bustle, confusion.
Fouth—abundance, plenty.
Fow—full, drunk.
Frae—from.
Freits—frights, ill omens, superstitious notions; "them leuks to freits,"&c., *those to whom things appear ominous will always be followed by frightful things.*
Froe—from.
Fu'—full.
Fuds, fud—a hare or rabbit's tail.
Fule—a fool.
Fumart—a pole cat.
Furich, furichinish—*see* Fourugh.
Furme—a form or bench.
Fun'—found.

GLOSSARY.

Furlet, firlot—a corn measure; the fourth part of a boll.
Fusion, foison—spirit, pith, flavour.
Fust—at rest.
Fut braid sawin'—corn sufficient to sow a foot breadth; or a foot breadth of ground on which one may sow. —*Lord Hailes.*
Fyl'd—fouled.

Gab—the mouth.
Gabbin'—chatting, idle prating.
Gaberlunzie—a wallet that hangs on the side or loins. So in Sir David Lyndsay's "Satyre of the thrie estaits," Edin. 1602, *Beir ze that bag upon zour lunzie.*
Gaberlunzie-man—a wallet man or tinker, who appears to have been formerly a jack-of-all-trades.
Gade—went.
Gae—go, gave.
Gaed, gae'd—went.
Gaid—went.
Gaif—gave.
Gain—"gain ye," *last you.*
Gainsays—denies, contradicts (sub. *it.*)
Gain-stands—opposes.
Gait—a road-way; "to the gait," *gone off;* "to tak the gait," *to depart.*
Gane—gone, overtaken.
Gang, ganging—go, going.
Gappocks—morsels, mouthfuls.
Gar—cause, force, compel.
Gardies—the arms; sing. Gardy.
Garse—grass.
Gart—caused, made, compelled.
Gat—begot.
Gate—a way, lane, gait, gesture.
Gates—ways.
Gaun, gawn—going; "gaun to," *about to.*
Gear—wealth, property, goods of any kind; "head-gear," *head dress.*
Geck'd—flouted, mocked; *gecking* is, casting up the head in derision.
Ged hame—went home.
Gee—give.

Gee—the pet, sulks.
Geid—gave.
Ghaist—ghost.
Gi, gie—give; gie'd—gave; gies—gives.
Gimmers—ewe sheep under two years old.
Gimp—jimp, slender.
Gin—given.
Gin—if, but.
Girdle—a circular plate of iron for baking cakes over the fire.
Girnels—large chests for holding meal.
Gither—"the gither," *together;* "a' the gither," *altogether.*
Glaked, glaiked—idle, foolish, frolicsome.
Glamer, glamour—charm, spell; the supposed influence of a charm on the eye, causing it to see objects differently from what they really are.
Gleed, gley'd—squint-eyed.
Glen—a narrow valley between mountains.
Glent, glint—shine, glitter, glance.
Gleyd—an old horse; "ane crukit gleyd fell our ane huch," *a lame old horse fell over a cliff.—Bannatyne Poems.*
Glie—glee, mirth.
Glift—glistened, glittered; a sight by chance.
Gloamin, gloming—twilight, fall of evening.
Gloom—frown, scowl.
Glowming—*see* Gloamin.
Glowr, glour—a frown, stern look.
Glowran, glowrin'—looking intensely.
Glowr'd—stared broadly.
Gluve—"to play at the gluve," *to play at the glove tilt.*
Gnidge—to pinch, or rub off, press, squeeze.
God's-pennie—earnest money to bind the bargain.
Gouke—simpleton; from *gowk,* the cuckoo.
Goodman—husband, master of the house; "the goodman of day,"*the sun.*
Goodwife—wife, mistress of the house.

GLOSSARY.

Gooshets, gushets—stocking clocks.
Goud—gold.
Gowan—field-daisy. *Bellis perennis.*
Gowd—gold.
Gowden—golden.
Gowdspink—goldfinch.
Gowff'd—struck; a metaphor from the game of *golf;* a sort of rustic tennis.
Grain'd—groaned.
Graif—grave.
Graith—furniture, accoutrements.
Graith'd—"gowden-graith'd," *trapped,* or *caparisoned with gold.*
Grat—cried, wept.
Gree—agree.
Gree—prize, pre-eminence, superiority.
Greet—to weep, cry like a child.
Greiting—weeping, tears.
Grite—*see* Greet.
Grots, groats—oats with the husks taken off.
Groat—a silver coin, first struck by David II. A proverbial name for a small sum.
Gryce—a pig.
Gude, guid—good.
Gudeman, guidman—*see* Goodman.
Gudewife—*see* Goodwife.
Guss, guse—a goose.
Gutcher—grandfather, goodsire.
Gyles—guiles.

Ha'—hall.
Hacket-kail—hashed coleworts.
Ha'd, haud—hold; "ha'd us in pottage," *hold* or *keep us in pottage;* "haud awa'," *hold away.*
Hadden—holden.
Hads—holds, keeps.
Hae—have; "hae, there's your faith and throth, Willie;" "hold," *tenez.*
Haff, haflens—half.
Haggize, haggis—a pudding made of a sheep's pluck, mixed with suet and oatmeal, boiled in the stomach of the animal; a favourite dish in Scotland.

Hail—whole.
Hair-mould—mouldy, hoar or white with mould.
Hald, hauld—hold, habitation, fortress.
Hale-sale—wholesale.
Halesom—wholesome, healthful.
Hallan-shaker—a ragamuffin, sturdy beggar. According to Ramsay "a hallan" is a fence, built of stone, turf, or a movable flake of heather, at the sides of the door in country places, to defend them from the wind. The trembling attendant, he adds, about a forgetful great man's gate or levee, is all expressed in the term "hallen-shaker." It may, however, with equal probability, be derived from *haillons* (rags) Fr.
Haper-Gallic—Gaelic, Erse. "Aber Gaelik," *speak Irish.*—Crawford's Notes on Buchanan, p. 15.
Happers—hoppers of mills.
Happity leg—lame leg.
Harn sheet—coarse linen cloth, used among the poorer people for shirts and sheets. Properly Hardin, hardyn—cloth made of the *hards* or refuse of flax.
Haud—*see* Had.
Haughs—valleys, or low grounds on the sides of rivers.
Hauss-bane—collar-bone, throat.
Hawick gill—a half mutchkin; double the ordinary gill.
Hawkit—white-faced.
Haws—*see* Haughs.
Haws'd her—took her about the neck, embraced her.
Heal—whole.
Heartsome—happy, merry, cheerful.
Hecht, heght—promised, engaged.
Heeze—to lift up, raise.
Heezy—a hoist; a toss, such as one gets in a rough sea.
Heid, heidit—behead, beheaded.
Heiden-hill—the place of execution; the beheading-hill.

Heir—inherit.
Hek, heck—rack, out of which the cattle eat their hay or straw.
Hellim—helm, rudder.
Hether, heather—heath, ling; heather, is *calluna vulgaris:* heath, *Erica*, of different sorts.
Heyd—hyed.
Hight—promised.
Hind—beyond; "far hind," *far beyond:* "far-hie-an'-atour," *at a considerable distance.—Aberd.*
Hinny—honey.
Hint, ahint—behind.
Hirples—halts, walks lame.
His—has.
Hobbil—to cobble, patch, mend clumsily.
Hoggers—coarse stockings without feet.
Holt—a wood; also barren, hilly ground.
Hool, hule—husk, hull.
Hooly—softly, slowly.
Host—to cough.
Hough, hoch—the thigh, the brawn of the leg.
How, howe—a hollow place.
How—hollow.
Howms, holms—level, low, sheltered ground on the banks of a river.
Hugh, heugh, heuch—a crag, precipice, ragged steep.
Hund—hound; "hund the tykes," *incite the dogs to keep the sheep together.*
Hunder—hundred.
Hurklen—crouching.
Hussy'fskap—housewifery, housewifeship.
Hynd, hyne—peasant, rustic labourer.

Ilfardly—ill-favouredly, after an ugly fashion.
Ilk, ilka—each, every.
Ingle—fire; "ingle-side," *fireside.*
ngraff—engrave.

Insight, insicht—household furniture, in-door stock.
Into—in.
Irie—afraid of apparitions.
Irks—feels uneasy or distressed.
Ise—I shall.
Ither—other, each other.

Jack, jak—a fencible jacket, made with thin pieces of iron quilted in. "By 87th statute, parliament 6 James V. it was provided that *yeamen* have *jackes* of *plate*."—*Lord Hailes.*
Jag—the best part of calf-leather.
Jak—*see* Jack.
Japin'—jesting, jeering, mocking, foolish talk.
Jaw—pour, throw out a quantity of water with a jerk.
Jee'd—moved to one side.
Jenkin's hen—"to die like," *to die unmarried.*
Jimp—neat, slender, tight.
Jo—sweetheart, whether male or female.
Jow—jowl, jolt, knell. Mr Burns justly observes that this word "includes both the swinging motion and pealing sound of a large bell."
Jooks—love bows.
Jupe—a short mantle or cloak for a woman.

Kail, kale—the herb called colewort; much used in Scotland for pottage.
Kail, kale—broth made with vegetables in it, especially colewort.
Kail-yard—a kitchen garden.
Kain, cane—a duty, besides rent, paid by a tenant to his landlord, such as hens, ducks, cheese, and other articles for the use of his table; "sair he paid the kane," will therefore mean *he suffered more grievously than others:* was treated with particular severity.
Kame, kaim—a comb.

GLOSSARY.

Kebbuck—a cheese, generally one of a large size.
Keek, keik—to peep, look; a stolen glance.
Keeking-glass—looking-glass.
Keel, keil—red ochre.
Ken—to know, to be acquainted with.
Kenn'd, kent—knew, known.
Keepit—kept.
Keil—*see* Keel.
Kent—a long staff used by shepherds for leaping over ditches.
Kimmer—a gossip, gudewife, married woman; *commere*, Fr.
Kinnen, cuning—a rabbit.
Kirk—church.
Kirn—churn.
Kirtles—upper petticoats.
Kist—chest; "kist fu' o whistles," *the organ*.
Kit—a small wooden vessel, hooped and staved.
Kith and kin—acquaintance and kindred.
Kye, ky—cows.
Kin'—sort, race.
Knak—to taunt, mock, or jest.
Knockit beer—barley stripped of the husk by being beaten in a hollow stone with a maul.
Knowe—knoll, hillock.
Kog—*see* Cog.
Kuill—cool.
Kurchis—*see* Curches.
Kyrtle—waist and petticoat.
Kyth—*see* Kith.
Kythed—shown, made manifest.

Lack—want.
Ladses—lads; a sort of double plural.
Lag—hindmost.
Laid—load.
Laigh, laich—low, hollow; low field which has been taken in from a marsh or moss.
Lain, lane—alone; "a' my lain," *all alone;* "ye're your lain," *you're alone;* "nane but her lain," *none but herself*.
Laird—landholder, proprietor of land or houses.
Lairie—marshy, boggy, muddy.
Luith—loth.
La'lands—lowlands, low country; the south, the south-west, east, and south-east parts of Scotland, where the English language prevails, are called Lowlands, in contradistinction to the Highlands, of which the common speech is the Gaelic.
Land'arttown—inland country village.
Lane—*see* Lain.
Lang—to long; langs, *longs*.
Lang-kail—pottage made of coleworts.
Langer—longer.
Langest—longest.
Lap—leaped.
Lapper'd milk—coagulated milk; milk become sour and clotted by long keeping.
Lapwing—the grey plover.
Lauch'd—laughed.
Lauchters—laughs.
Laugh, lauch—law.
Lave—the remainder, the rest.
Laverok, laverock—the lark.
Law—low.
Lawin—the tavern reckoning.
Lawing-free—Scot-free.
Lay—allay, alleviate.
Leal, leil—loyal, honest, true, upright.
Lear'd—learned, acquired.
Lea, lee—ground uncropped, or in pasture; "lily-white lea," *pasture white with daisies and trefoil*.
Leech—physician.
Leel—*see* Leal.
Leese me, leeze me—used when one loves, or is pleased with anything.
Leglin, leglen—milking-pail, generally one of the staves projects to form the handle.
Leigh—low.
Leighlands—lowlands.
Leir—learning.

Lemanless—without lover or husband.
Lemman, lemmune, lemane—sweetheart.
Lenno, laeno—child. Gael. *leanobh.*
Leuch, leugh—laughed.
Lever—sooner, rather.
Lick—a wag, one who plays on another.
Lift—firmament, atmosphere.
Lig—to lie, recline.
Liges—lieges, subjects.
Lilt—to sing cheerfully.
Liltin'—dancing to music, merry-making.
Limmers — sluts, or (more properly) bitches, a species of dog being anciently so called; an opprobrious term applied to young women, expressive of displeasure, but not implying immorality of conduct.
Linkin'—walking quickly, tripping.
Lincome-twine, linkum twine—pack-thread.
Lintwhite—linnet.
Lit—dye, colour.
Lithe—to listen, attend.
Loake, lock—a small quantity, a handful.
Loaning, loan—an opening between fields left uncultivated for the sake of driving the cattle homewards; where also the cattle are frequently milked.
Loch—lake. [silent.
Loddin, lowden, loan, lown—quiet,
Lo'e—love; lo'ed—loved.
Loo, loo'd—*see* Lo'e.
Loon—rogue, worthless fellow.
Loos'd—set off, began the battle.
Loot—let, suffered.
Losel—idle rascal, worthless wretch.
Loun—*see* Loon.
Loup—leap.
Lourd—rather; "I rather lourd," might be rendered, *I had much rather.*
Lout—stoop, bow down; "louted her down," *she stooped down.*
Low—blaze, flame.

Lown—*see* Loon; *see also* Loddin.
Lowns—is lown, calm, serene.
Luck—to have good or bad fortune. Also to enclose or shut up.
Lucken—close, growing closely together, or closely joined to one another.
Luckengowan — the globe flower. *Trollius Europæus.*
Lucky young—too young.
Lue—love; lued—loved.
Lugs—ears.
Luik—look.
Luk—*see* Lout.
"I zern full fane
To luk my head, and sit doun by zou."
I earnestly long to sit down at your side. Luk is here evidently printed for Lout, *to stoop.*
Lurdanes—worthless persons, whether men or women.
Luve—love; Luver—lover.
Lyart—having grey hairs intermixed.
Lyth—calm, shelter, shade, protected either from the blast or sunshine.

Mabbies—mabs, mobs, caps, head-dress for women.
Mae—more.
Mae—the bleat of a lamb.
Maik—mate, fellow, marrow, like.
Main'd meaned.
Mair—more.
Maist—most.
Mait—might.
Mane—moan.
Mang—"like to mang," *like to become frantic.*
Marrow—mate, companion, associate.
Maskene-fatt—mashing-vat, a large vessel used in brewing.
Maskin-pat—tea-pot.
Ma't—malt.
Mat—might.
Maukin—hare.
Maun—must.
Maunna—must not.
Maut—malt.

Mavis—thrush.
Mawking—hare.
May—maid, young woman.
Mazer dish—a drinking cup of maple. The original is "ezar," which may be *Acer* the *Maple*.
Meal-kail—soup with pot-herbs and oatmeal.
Mease—mess, *i.e.*, to make up the number four.
Meikle—much.
Meil-sek—meal-sack.
Meise—move, soften, mollify.
Mel, mell—meddle, interfere.
Mense—grace, decorate.
Menzie—company, retinue, followers.
Merk—mark, a Scotish silver coin—value, sterling, *thirteen shillings and fourpence*.
Meshanter—misadventure, disaster.
Mickle—much.
Milk-bowie—milk-bowl, wooden vessel into which ewes are milked.
Milk-syth—milk-strainer.
Mill, mull—snuff-horn, snuff-box.
Minny, minnie—mother.
Minstrels—musicians, fiddlers, pipers.
Mirk—dark; "in the mirk," *in darkness*.
Mishanter—*see* Meshanter.
Mister—need, necessity; "their mister," *what they need or want, the necessaries of life*. Menestér, Sp.
Mither—mother.
Mittans, mittens—woollen or worsted gloves.
Mizlie-chinned—variegated in colour, as if from fire or burning.
Moggans—long sleeves for a woman's arms, wrought like stockings.
Mony—many.
Mote—might; "what mote bee," *what it might be*.
Mou—mouth.
Mought—might.
Mucked—cleansed; applied to a cow-house or stable.
Muckle—much; also great, large.

Mudie—bold.
Muir—moor.
Mun—must.
Mutches—linen coifs or caps for women.
Mutchkin—a liquid measure, equal to an English pint.
Mysell—myself.

Na—no, not.
Nae—none.
Naething—nothing.
Nainsell—own self.
Nane—none.
Neep—turnip.
Neest—next.
Neez—nose.
Neigartes—niggards.
Nicher—neigh.
Niest—next.
Nocht—nought.
Nok—button of a spindle.
Nor—than.
Norland—north, northern.
Norse—Norway.
Norss—Norways.
Notour—notorious.
Nought—nothing.
Nout-feet—neats' feet, cow-heels.
Nurice-fee—nurse's fee.

O'—of.
Obraid—upbraid.
O'er—over.
'Oman—woman.
Ony—any.
Or—ere, before.
Orisons—prayers.
Our—over.
Out-shinn'd—bow-legged.
Out-sight—out of doors goods or stock.
Owr, owre—over; "owr-word," *burthen of a song*.
Owrlay—cravat.
Owsen—oxen.
Oxter—arm-pit; "in his oxter," *under his arm*.

Pa—paw, hand.
Pa'—*see* Paw.
Pack—gang, parcel of people.
Paction—contract, agreement.
Padell—a small leathern-bag or wallet.
Paiks—chastisement ; " got their paiks," *got well beat.*
Parridge, parritch—porridge made of oatmeal.
Partons, partans—the common sea crab.
Pat—pot.
Pat—put.
Paunches—tripe.
Paw—step or dance. Pas, Fr.
Pawky—sly, shrewd, cunning, knowing.
Pearl blue—light blue.
Pearling, pearlins—thread lace.
Peat-pat—the hole from which peat is dug.
Peat-creel—a wicker basket in which peats are carried.
Pens—plumes, finery.
Peshaw—show.
Philabeg—kilt, the short petticoat worn by Highlandmen.
Phraze—noise, fuss.
Pibrochs—martial tunes, peculiar to the Highlanders, composed to suit the bagpipes ; of which see a fine and curious description in Dr Beattie's "Essays on Laughter and Ludicrous Composition" (a note).
Pickle—a small quantity, consisting of different particles combined ; also a grain of corn, or single seed of any kind.
Pickles—small quantities.
Pinners—caps with lappets, formerly worn by women of rank.
Pint-stoup—a tin measure containing two quarts.
Pith—strength, might, force.
Placads—placards, public announcements.
Plack—a Scotish coin, value two bodals (Bothwells), or fourpence Scotish, *i.e.*, the third of a penny English.
Plaidie, plaid—a piece of checkered and generally variegated stuff worn by women as a hood and shawl combined.
Plaiden, plaiding—a coarse woollen cloth.
Plak—*see* Plack.
Playand—playing.
Pled—pleaded.
Pleen—complain.
Plenishing—household furniture ; also the stock of a farm.
Plett—plaited.
Plouckie-fac'd—pimpled.
Pluche—plough.
Pock, poke—bag.
Pockpuds—poke puddings, a name of derision given to the English from the idea that they are fond of good living.
Polk—bag, sack.
Pou—pull ; Pou'd—pulled.
Pow-sodie—sheep's-head broth.
" Praise be blest" (page 243), a familiar expression is used by the common people in London, "Thanks be praised," *nonsense to avoid profaneness.*
Press—throng, heat of battle.
Prick'd—spurred.
Pri'd, pried, priv'd—tasted, tried, proved.
Prie—taste, try, prove.
Priving—provender.
Progues—brogues, Highland shoes, made of the raw hide.
Protch—brooch.
Protty—pretty, bonnie.
Pu'd—pulled ; Pu'ing—pulling.
Puddy—a kind of silk stuff ; Paduasoy.
Putted—threw ; "putted the stane," *threw the stone,* a country game.

Quarters—lodgings.
Quat—quit, quitted.
Quey—heifer, or young cow.

GLOSSARY.

Quha—who.
Quhairfor—wherefore.
Quhat—what.
Quhaten, quhaten a—what, what a.
Quheit—wheat.
Quhen—when.
Quher—where.
Quhilk—which.
Quhittil—knife.
Quhyle—while.
Quod—quoth, say, says, said.

Rade—rode.
Raip—rope.
Ramukloch—to change one's tune from mirth to sadness
Randy—a scold; appropriated to a female.
Rang—reigned.
Rant—to be jovial in a noisy way.
Ranted—talked loud, made noisy mirth.
Rantin'—exhilarating; "a ranting fire," *a roaring fire*.
Rantry-tree—rowan tree, the mountain ash, which was believed to be a preservative against witchcraft.
Ranty-tanty—the broad-leaved sorrel, *Rumex acetosella*, which was boiled with colewort and beat up together.
Rawe—a row of houses.
Rax—to reach, stretch; "rax the rout," *strike the blow*.
Ream—cream.
Reave—bereave.
Reck—care; "what recks," *what signifies*.
Red-coats—English soldiers.
Rede—advice.
Rede—to advise.
Reek—smoke; "reeking-het," *smoking hot*.
Reft—bereft.
Regal—regale.
Reill—reel on which the yarn was wound while being spun.
Remead—remedy.
Renze—reins.

Revers—robbers, pirates, banditti.
Rin—run.
Ring—reign.
Ringle-eyed—having a great proportion of white in the eye, wall-eyed.
Rive—split, burst.
Rok, rock—distaff.
Rokely, rokelay—a short cloak.
Rosts—roasts, anything requiring to be broiled.
Row—roll, wrap; Row'd—wrapped.
Rowth—plenty, abundance.
Rude—rood, cross.
Rullions—brogues or shoes made from the raw hide, when taken from the beast, and shaped to the feet without other preparation. Coarse-made, masculine women.
Runkled—wrinkled.
Ruse—boast; "toom ruse," *empty boast*.
Ryal—royal.
Ryfarts—radishes.

Sae—so.
Saft—soft; Saftly—softly.
Sair—sore; Sarely—sorely.
Sakeless—innocent.
Sall—shall.
Sald—sold; "sald by kind," *sold by the sort or name*.
Samen—same.
Sangs—songs.
Sappy—juicy.
Sark—shirt; "sark of God," *surplice*.
Sarked—provided with shirts or shifts.
Saucht—quiet, at ease, in peace.
Saul—soul.
Saut—salt.
Saw—saying, maxim, proverbial expression.
Scadlips—broth with only a small quantity of barley in it, and on this account apt to burn the mouth.
Scale, skail—spill, spread, disperse.
Scant—scarce, scarcity, penurious.
Scantly—scarcely, hardly.
Scheit—sheet.

GLOSSARY.

Schene—sheen, shining.
Schiples—shipless, without a ship.
Scho—shee.
Schone—shoes,
Schro—beshrew, curse; "I schro the lyar fu' leis me zow," *curse you for* (a) *liar, I love you heartily.—Lord Hailes.*
Schuke—shook.
Schule—shovel.
Schynand—shining.
Scornfu'—scornful.
Scraps—scrapes.
Scrimped—poor, mean, bare.
Scrimpit—narrow, contracted, covetous, scant allowance.
Scuds—brisk beer, foaming ale.
Scuff—brush, to go or walk softly as if scarcely to touch the ground.
Scull—a shallow basket, sometimes used as a cradle.
Seim—semblance.
Sel, sell—self.
Sen—since.
Se'nteen—seventeenth.
Sess—taxes.
Seugh, seuch—furrow, ditch.
Sey—"greensey apron," *a kind of woollen stuff.*
Seyd—essayed, tried.
Shanks-legs; "rade on gude shanks naggie," *a cant phrase for walked.*
Shath-mont, schaftmon—a measure of six inches in length, the fist closed with the thumb extended.
Shaw—a wood, woody bank.
Shearing—reaping.
Shears—scissors.
Sheene—"silken sheene," *shining silk.*
Shoene—shoes.
Shent—hurt, confounded.
Shield, shiel'—a slight or temporary erection by shepherds on the mountains, for the convenience in summer of attending to their flocks.
Shimmer'd — shone; Shimmering—shining.
Shog—jog, shake.

Shoo—shoe; "so ill to shoo," *so difficult to please,* a metaphor from the smith's shop.
Shoon—shoes.
"Shot the lock"—put back the bolt; opened the door.
Shug—to rock.
Shure—shore, reaped, sheared.
Shute—shout.
Shyre—"as shyre a lick," *as clean a cheat:* properly, clear, pure.
Sic—such.
Sicht—sighed.
Sick, sickan, sicken, sike—such.
Sike—a little rill or rivulet, usually dry in summer.
Siker, sicker—sure, secure, firm.
Siklike—suchlike.
Silder—silver.
Siller—silver, money, *l'argent.*
Sindle—seldom.
Sine—"sinsyne," *since then.*
Sith—since.
Skaith—hurt, damage.
Skair—scare, fright.
Skant—*see* Scant.
Skerss—scarce.
Skink—broth made of shins of beef.
Skinkled—sparkled.
Skipper—master of a small vessel.
Sklaif—slave.
Slaes—sloes.
Slaid—slew.
Slaited—wiped, whetted.
Slee—sly.
Slim—a person that cannot be trusted.
Smoor, smore—smother.
Smurtl'd—smirked, laughed in a suppressed way.
Smyless—smileless, dejected, sorrowful.
Snae, snaw—snow.
Sned—to cut, lop off.
Sneevling—one who speaks through the nose.
Snell—keen, sharp, severe.
Sneeshin', sneezing, snishing—snuff. Ramsay suggests that it may mean

GLOSSARY. 571

"contentment, a husband, love, money," &c.
Snood—a head-band or ribband for tying up the hair, worn only by single women.
Snout—nose.
Soddin—seethed, enough boiled or stewed.
Sodgers—soldiers.
Soud—should.
Soughing—sighing, the peculiar sound made by the wind among trees.
Soums—a term expressing quantity of sheep : a soum means five, in some places ten sheep.
Sounding—blowing his horn.
Soup, sup—a spoonful, a small quantity.
Souple—flexible, swift, nimble, cunning.
Sowens—flummery made of the dust of oatmeal remaining amongst the seeds (husks) steeped until soured, the liquor is then boiled to a consistency, and eaten with milk or butter.
Sow-libber—sow-gelder.
Soy—silk.
Spack—spake.
Spear—see Speir.
Speel'd—climbed, clumb.
Speer—see Speir.
Speere—a hole in the wall of a house through which the family received and answered the inquiries of strangers, without being under the necessity of opening the door or window.
Speir—to ask, to inquire, or search out.
Speldens—white fish split up, salted, and dried in the sun.
Spier'd—asked.
Spill—spoil, destroy.
Spindles and whorles—implements used in spinning with the distaff.
Spiogs—branches of oak from which the bark has been peeled for tanner's use. Supposed to mean the arms (see p. 262).
Splee-fitted—splay-footed.
Spring—tune.
Spurtill, spurtle—a circular stick, with which porridge, broth, &c., are stirred when being boiled.
Stack—a rick of grain or peats.
Stanc'd—stationed.
Stank—large pond or pool of standing water.
Staw—stole.
Stean, stane—stone.
Stended—stalked, moved with long steps.
Steeks—closes, shuts.
Steeks—stitches.
Steer—stir, meddle, or injure.
Stent—stop, cease.
Stenze—page 267.
Stilt—crutch, the handle of a plough.
Sting—see note, p. 316.
Stint—stopped, paused.
Stirk—a young bull.
Stocks—heads of cabbage or colewort.
Stoup—a deep and narrow vessel for holding liquids ; measures for sale of spirits, such as gill-stoups, pint-stoups, &c.
Stoup, stoupe—a prop, support.
Stoure, stoor—dust (in motion).
Stoun, stown—stolen.
Strae—straw ; "had fair strae death tane her awa'," *had she died a natural death.*
Straif—strove.
Straiks, straks—strokes.
Strake, straked—struck.
Strick—strict.
Sturt—trouble, vexation.
Sune—soon.
Sussie, sussy—care, anxiety, trouble.
Sutor, souter, soutar—a shoemaker.
Suthron (southern)—English.
Swaird—grassy surface of the ground.
Swankies—swainkins, clever young fellows.

Swaets, swaits, swats—new ale, small ale.
Swak *away*—decay, consume, waste.
Swapped—exchanged.
Swats—*see* Swaets.
Swear, sweer, sweir—averse, backward, unwilling.
Swith—quickly.
Sybows—young onions.
Syke—*see* Sike.
Syne—after, after that, afterward, then; "sune as syne," *soon as late.*

Ta'en, tain—taken.
Tait, teats—a small quantity or portion.
Tak—take.
Taken—token.
Tald—told.
Tane—the one; Tither—the other.
Tangle—sea-weed, *Laminaria.*
Tap—top; Tap-knots—bunches of ribbons worn on a woman's cap or bonnet.
Tappit-hen—the Scotish quart stoup; so called from a small knob (tap or top) on the lid peculiar to that vessel; also hens called in England copped, or crested, being in Scotland called tapped or topped hens.
Targats—tassels.
Tarrow—delay, feel reluctant.
Tarry woo—wool of sheep that have been tarred.
Tartan—a sort of pudding made with red colewort chopped small, and mixed with oatmeal.
Tartan—a plaiding, cross striped or checkered stuff of various colours, worn by the Highlanders, each clan having its particular pattern and colourings. Tartan-plaid, tartan-screen—a large piece of this worn by the women over their head and shoulders.
Tarveal—plague, fretfully torment, or fatigue.
Tashed—stained, spoiled.

Tauld—told.
Teats—*see* Tait.
Tees'd—went slowly.
Teddin'—spreading out.
Tedder, tether—a rope with which a horse is tied, to limit his ground at pasture.
Temper-pin—the wooden pin used for regulating the motion of a spinning-wheel.
Tent—heed.
Tenty—heedful, cautious.
Thae—these, those.
Thairs—there is.
Thegither—together.
The-night—to-night; The-day—to-day.
Thee—thrive, prosper.
Thift—theft.
Thimber—gross, heavy, inflated.
Thir—these.
Thocht—thought; Thochts—thoughts.
Thole, thoill—suffer, endure, bear.
Thou's, thouse—thou shalt.
Thrang—busy.
Thrangs—throngs, crowds, presses.
Thraw—twist, twine, turn, cross, thwart.
Thraw-cruk—an instrument used by husbandmen for twisting hay or straw into ropes.
Thrawis—throes, pangs, agonies.
Thristles—thistles.
Thrummy—a gown or petticoat so worn at the bottom as to appear fringed.
Thud—stroke, noise or sound occasioned by a blow, or the fall of any heavy body.
Tiff—good order.
Tift—the action of the wind when it lifts in the air dust, straw, &c.
Till—to.
Tinclair—tinker.
Tine—to lose, die.
Tinkler—tinker.
Tipenny, tiponny—twopenny; ale sold for twopence a Scotish pint.
Tirled—"tirle at the pin," *twirled the*

latch, attempted to open the door.
Tither—other.
Titter—rather, sooner.
Titty—sister.
Tocher—marriage-portion, fortune.
Todlin', todlen—toddling, walking like a child or old person, with short steps in a tottering way.
Tone—the one.
Toofal—"ere the toofal of the night," *before nightfall;* an image, Mr Lambe thinks, drawn from a suspended canopy, so let fall as to cover what is below.
Toom—empty; toom'd, emptied.
Tosh—tight, neat.
Tother—the other.
Touk of drum—sound of drum, beat of drum.
Tow—flax in a prepared state.
"Tow me owre the wa'," *let me over the wall by a rope.*
Toys—head-dresses, anciently worn
Travelling—travailing, in labour.
Trene—wooden.
Trews — Highland pantaloons, breeches and stockings all of one piece.
Triest forth—"appoint forth," *draw forth by assignation.*
Troch—trough.
Troth—truth; applied to faith between lovers, pledged by means of a symbol.
Trouze—trews, sometimes used for stockings only.
Trow—believe, to trust to, to confide in.
Trows—*see* Trews.
Truncheour—trencher.
Tul, tull—to.
Turs—as much heath as a horse can carry on his back, a truss.
Twa—two.
Twal—twelve.
Twche—tough.
Tweel—twill, cloth woven so as to make the warp threads appear diagonal.
Twin—to part, to separate.
Twin'd—parted; Twin'd of—deprived of.
Twirtle twist; p. 486.
Tyke—dog.
Tyne—to lose, die.

Uder—other.
Unco'—very; also strange, wonderful, uncouth.
Uneasy—difficult.
Unkend—unknown.
Unmufit, unmuvit—unmoved, undisturbed.
Unsonsie—unlucky.
Upo'—upon.

Valziant—valiant.
Vaunty—boastful.
Vow—*see* Wow.

Wad—would; Wadna—would not.
Wad—a pledge; "a wad," *in pawn.*
Wae—woe; "wae worth ze," *woe be with you, woe befall ye.*
Waefu', waeful—woeful.
Waes me—woe is me.
Waik—weak.
Wald—weld, join.
Wale—choose.
Wale—"the wale," *the choice, the best.*
Wallowit—wan, faded.
Waly, waly—an exclamation of grief, sorrow, &c.
Wame—belly.
Wan—got, won, gained.
Wan—pale.
Wan chansie—unlucky.
Wandoghts—silly, weak, puny creatures.
Wan water—some sort of cordial, drunk for restoring the colour to pale or fainting persons.
War—worse.

War—"war them a'," *fight or beat them all.*
Warde—warn, advise.
Ware—bestow, spend.
Wark—work.
Warld—world ; "Warlds," *times.*
Wat—wet.
Wat, wate—trow, know, believe.
Water-stoups—conical wooden vessels in which water is fetched or kept.
Wauk—walk.
Wauken—waken.
"Waukin' o' the fauld"—the act of watching the sheep-fold, about the end of summer, when the lambs were weaned, and the ewes milked.
Waur—worse.
Wayward—perverse, headstrong.
Weaponshaw—show of arms or weapons, a sort of militia review.
Wear—drive, gather.
Wearifu'—wearisome, vexatious.
Weary—wearisome, disagreeable; also vexed, sorrowful.
Wecht—weight ; an implement used in winnowing. It resembles a sieve in form, but the bottom is made of skin or canvas, and not perforated.
Wed—"to wed," *to pawn.*
Weddeen—a wedding.
Wee—little ; "Wee bit," *little piece:* "Wee, wee," *very little;* "A wee," *a short time.*
Weel—well.
Weel-fared, weel-faur'd—well-favoured, handsome.
Ween—think.
Weerd—fortune, fate.
Weers—fears.
Weet—wet, rain.
Weir—war.
Weit—with't, with it.
Welt—wet.
West!in'—west, western.
Wexed—waxed, grew, became.
Wha—who.
Whase—whose.
Whang—large slice.

What recks—what matters, or signifies.
What an a—what, what kind of a.
Whigs—enemies to the Government before the Revolution, and friends to it since ; Presbyterians, Williamites, Hanoverians.
Whilk—which.
Whinging—whining.
Whorles—*see* Spindles.
Wicht—wight, man.
Wicht—strong.
Wid—would.
Widdershines—contrary to the course of the sun ; "Of a widdershines grow," *that grows backward, the wrong way.*
Widow—widower.
Wie—little ; "the wie thing I hae, *the little matter I possess.*
Wilily—slyly, cunningly.
Wilks—periwinkles.
Wiltu—wilt thou.
Win—get; "sal never win aboon't ava'," *will never get the better of it at all.*
Winna—will not.
Winsome—comely, agreeable, engaging.
Wis—trow, know, believe, think ; there is no modern word perfectly synonymous or equivalent.
Wiss—wish.
Wist — known, thought, believed, wished.
Wit—know.
Withershins—*see* Widdershines.
Wittin—known.
Won'd—lived, dwelled.
Wons—lives, dwells.
Woo'—wool.
Wood, wud—furious, mad ; "woodwroth," *furiously wrathful.*
Wordy—worthy.
Worries—chokes, suffocates.
Wow—woo.
Wow—"O wow! O wow!" an exclamation implying sometimes eagerness, sometimes wonder.

GLOSSARY.

Wrack—wreck.
Wraith—ghost, spirit, apparition.
Wrang—wriggle.
Wratacks—rickety persons, persons unable to walk as they should do; dwarfs.
Wreath—*see* Wraith.
Wreath of snow—a snowdrift, a heap of snow blown up by the wind.
Wun—live, dwell.
Wyle—entice.
Wylie—cunning.
Wyte—blame.

Yade—mare.
Yates—gates.
Yeed, yede—went.
Ye'r—your.

Ye's—you shall.
Yestreen—yesternight.
Yle—isle.
Yonker—young man.

Z.

This letter at the beginning of a syllable has the power of *y*, in the middle of one, before a consonant, that of *gh*.
Ze—ye.
Zou—you.
Zour—your.
Zeir—year.
Zit—yet.
Zule—Christmas, Yule.
Zung—young.

ERRATA.

In the Historical Essay, page 66, it is said that "The dialect he (Alexander Ross) uses is the broad Buchans," which proves to be a mistake. It is the vulgar dialect of Angus.

Page 68.—That this gallant monarch was a musician is sufficiently ascertained. At the second meeting he had with his queen at Newbottle, after the company had drunk, "Incountynent the kinge begonne before hyr to play of the clary-cordes, and after of the lute, which pleasyd hyr varey much."—(*Leland's Collectanea*, 1770, iii. 284).

Page 152—7th line from bottom, *white-hause bane*, should be *white hauss-bane*.
Page 265—10th line from bottom, *sut braid fawin*, should be *fut braid sawin*.
Page 307—6th line of first stanza, *eelift* should be *eetist*.
Dyne, dine, page 560, add—again in "The cruel Sister," a ballad of the same kind—

 " O by there came a harper fine,
 That harped to the king *at dine*."

www.ingramcontent.com/pod-product-compliance
Lightning Source LLC
Chambersburg PA
CBHW022116230426
43672CB00008B/1401